My Name is Leon

Revision Guide

Charlotte Crouch

Quotations from Kit de Waal, *My Name is Leon* (2016)

Quotations from the text used with kind permission from Kit de Waal and her agent.

Cover Image © 2023 Garry Morris

Copyright © 2023 Charlotte Crouch

All rights reserved.

ISBN: 9798853485341

Imprint: Independently published

Contents

A   **1**   **Chapter Analysis**

1	Chapter 1	50	Chapter 22
3	Chapter 2	51	Chapter 23
6	Chapter 3	53	Chapter 24
8	Chapter 4	56	Chapter 25
11	Chapter 5	58	Chapter 26
13	Chapter 6	60	Chapter 27
16	Chapter 7	64	Chapter 28
18	Chapter 8	68	Chapter 29
20	Chapter 9	70	Chapter 30
22	Chapter 10	74	Chapter 31
25	Chapter 11	78	Chapter 32
26	Chapter 12	80	Chapter 33
28	Chapter 13	82	Chapter 34
31	Chapter 14	84	Chapter 35
35	Chapter 15	87	Chapter 36
37	Chapter 16	91	Chapter 37
39	Chapter 17	94	Chapter 38
43	Chapter 18	96	Chapter 39
46	Chapter 19	98	Chapter 40
47	Chapter 20	100	Chapter 41
49	Chapter 21	103	Chapter 42

B   **106**   **Contexts and Concepts**

- 106   Biographical Context: Kit de Waal
- 108   Racial Tensions
- 112   Attitudes towards the Irish
- 115   Cultural References
- 118   Literary Influences and Genre

C   **120**   **Character Profiles**

120	Character List	134	Sylvia
123	Leon	137	Tufty
127	Carol	141	Devlin
131	Maureen		

D   **144**   **Example Essay**

E   **149**   **Glossary**

*	**Essay Hints**
5	Writing Book Titles
6	Embedding Quotations- Using Square Brackets
19	Embedding Quotations- Speech within a quotation
24	Writing about character
36	Introductions
42	Tentative Language
55	Assessment Objectives
59	Planning
67	Analytical Verbs
79	Language, Form and Structure
83	Tone, Atmosphere and Mood
105	Conclusions
117	Writing about context
119	Discussing Genre
150	Writer's Methods

The purpose of this text:
This text is a study guide, intended to supplement your reading of *My Name is Leon*. You should have purchased and read a copy of Kit de Waal's *My Name is Leon* before using this study guide to support your understanding.

Note on Formatting:
- Key Terminology is underlined. A definition is provided at the end of the section, and in the glossary at the end.
- **Key Quotations** are in bold.
- ***Ambitious vocabulary*** *(challenging words)* are written in bold and italics, and a definition is provided afterwards.

A - Chapter Analysis

Chapter 1

Summary
- It's 2nd April, 1980, and Leon's baby brother has just been born.
- Carol, Leon's mum, goes for a cigarette rather than feeding the baby.
- We learn Leon and the baby have different fathers; Leon's father is black and the baby's is white. Leon has never met the baby's father.
- Leon is staying in Tina (his neighbour)'s flat, with her baby, who he calls Wobbly Bobby.

Analysis
The novel begins with Leon meeting his brother for the first time. Instantly, we see the <u>theme</u> of brotherly love, and get a hint of the bond that is established between Leon and Jake: when the nurse tells Leon to be '**careful**' as the baby is '**very precious**', it simply states '**but Leon already knows.**'

The nurse initially thinks that Leon is 10, but he's only 8 years and 9 months. The nurse replies: '**You're nice and big for your age. A right little man.**' Throughout the text, adults around Leon treat his as though he is much older because of his size, perhaps adding to the responsibility Leon feels about looking after his family. The need for Leon to after his brother is established when the nurse tells Carol that the baby needs feeding, and Carol says, '**Can I do it in a minute? Sorry, I was just going to the smoking room.**' From the <u>exposition</u> of the text, the reader can <u>infer</u> that Carol prioritises her own wishes above her children's needs.

As Leon looks after the baby, he lists off things about himself like the nurse suggests. We learn that they both have different fathers, and Leon has never met the baby's dad. We learn that Leon's father is '**dark brown**' and Leon sees himself as '**light brown**'- Leon is multiracial, whereas the baby and Carol are white.

When Carol returns, Leon asks if she still has a baby in her tummy. She says '**No more. [...] Just me and you and him. Always.**' This line is particularly ***poignant*** (emotional / distressing) as it is only 5 chapters later that Leon and the baby are separated from Carol as they are taken into foster care.

Leon goes to stay with his neighbour, Tina, in her *maisonette* *(a self-contained, two floored flat)*. When he's there, Leon sleeps on sofa cushions on the floor, with a baby blanket and coats piled on top. Leon perceives this as '**like a nest or a den'**, but as a reader we recognise that this is not an ideal bed for a child to stay in.

Tina has a baby called Bobby, who Leon calls Wobbly Bobby. When Leon is at Tina's, he has to call Tina '**Auntie Tina**' and Carol '**Mum'**, as well as eat at the table. We can infer that there aren't many conventional rules at Carol's house.

The last line of the chapter is another poignant moment: '**Sometimes, Tina's boyfriend comes, but when he sees Leon he always says "Again?" and Tina always says "I know."'** The reader realises that Leon often stays around Tina's house, even before the baby was born, and Tina and her boyfriend are getting tired of it.

Questions

1. What themes does de Waal introduce in Chapter 1 of the text?
2. Why do you think de Waal starts the novel with the moment of the baby's birth?
3. How are the characters of Leon, Carol, and Tina introduced? What *characteristics (features/qualities)* do they have?

Terminology
Character- A person in a literary work
Exposition- The opening of a novel, where information about key characters and settings is established.
Inference- A conclusion based on logic and reasoning. As a reader, we infer things from what the writer implies.
Theme- Underlying messages or deeper meanings that the writer explores in literary texts.

Chapter 2

Summary

- Carol brings the baby home, and Leon is clearly deeply in love with him.
- Carol keeps leaving Leon alone at home to look after the baby
- Tina comes around to see Carol, and Carol says she is feeling 'down'. Tina tells her to see a doctor, but Carol is reluctant. She explains the pills she's been prescribed give her nightmares.
- Carol tells Leon a story when he can't sleep. She reminds him of the importance of school, and how he needs to get a good education to thrive in the world.
- Carol says the baby's name is Jake, but Leon is upset as Carol promised him he could be called Bo from the TV show *Dukes of Hazzard*.

Analysis

When Carol brings the baby home, she and Leon sit on the floor and watch him. We realise the extent of Leon's *infatuation (deep love)* for the baby when '**All that day and the next day, the baby is like the television. Leon can't stop watching him.**' This simile shows how much Leon loves him.

The novel is written in third person limited point of view, and humour is introduced when Leon notices things like '**The baby has got a really small willy but big balls. Leon hoped the baby's willy will catch up.**' Although the novel has serious themes, it aims to address them in a light-hearted, non-preachy way. There are often moments like these where the tone shifts to humorous.

When talking to the baby, Leon introduces himself as '**Big. Brother. […] My. Name. Is. Leon. I am eight and three quarters. I am a boy.**' The theme of identity is made clear from this quotation which makes up the title of the text- this bildungsroman / coming-of-age story explores Leon's search for his own identity.

In school, Leon gives a talk to his peers about his new brother, claiming '**I'm the one in charge of my baby when mum's not there.**'

Particularly for a modern reader, this revelation is concerning, but the teachers don't seem to pick up on this. This may be a comment about the lack of safeguarding procedures in the 1980s.

However, we quickly see Leon's home life deteriorating: '**Carol says Leon can't go to school because it's too wet and rainy.**' She often leaves him with the baby to go to the phone box, but we don't know for a few chapters who she is trying to call. When Tina comes to visit, she lets herself in with a key, and '**Carol starts crying. She's always crying these days.**' We get hints that she suffered from postnatal depression after Leon- Carol tries to reassure Tina that '**It's not like last time. I just feel sort of down, you know**.' Tina keeps trying to persuade Carol to go to the doctors, but last time she went, she says '**they wanted me to go to some bloody centre twice a week**' and '**Them tablets give me nightmares.**'

We also hear more about Leon's father, Byron- he '**came round every day when Leon was a baby**' until he '**went inside**'- a colloquial term for being sent to prison. The information about Leon's father makes us question even more who the baby's father is.

That night, Carol tells Leon a story about a noisy boy who saved his village. Later in the text, we see Maureen and Sylvia tell Leon stories at night too, and this story seems to hint that Carol loves her son and wants him to be himself, but she isn't always able to teach him the right things. She reassures Leon he'll go the school the next day, but '**Carol says this every night but it's been five days since Leon went to school.**' Ironically, she then talks about the importance of getting a good education: '**If you don't go to school you won't learn anything, Leon. And if you don't learn anything you can't get a good job and a nice house and lots of toys.**'

At the end of the chapter, Leon refuses to kiss Carol back- '**She promised he could call the baby Bo from** *The Dukes of Hazzard*' but she instead called him Jake. *The Dukes of Hazzard* is a key motif in the novel- it is a TV comedy series about two close young male cousins, Bo and Duke, who (alongside other members of their family) try to evade the police as they get up to mischief. The show seems to be symbolic of a *fraternal* (brotherly) bond.

Questions

1. What evidence is there from this chapter that Carol is a good mother? What evidence is there that she is not fulfilling all the roles of being a good mother?
2. We often hear background information about Carol and the past as Leon overhears conversations. Why do you think this is?
3. Why do you think de Waal included the motif of The Dukes of Hazzard? What key themes and ideas does it emphasise?
4. Other motifs seen this chapter include Action Men and the phone box. What key themes or concepts might these emphasise or highlight?

Terminology

Colloquial- Chatty / conversational
Coming-of-Age- A genre (also known as a bildungsroman) which narrates the story of a protagonist from childhood to adulthood; immaturity to maturity; naivety to wisdom.
Irony- Using language that signals the opposite, usually for comedic or emphatic effect.
Motif- A feature, idea, or image that reoccurs throughout a text to develop other narrative elements such as theme or mood.
Simile- An indirect comparison, usually using 'like' or 'as' to compare the qualities of one thing to another.
Third Person Limited Point of View- The writer tells the story from the perspective of the protagonist; the reader sees the thoughts of the protagonist, but through the third person 'he' or 'she'.
Tone- The author's attitude towards a certain topic

Essay Hint- Writing Book Titles

When you're writing the title of a book in an essay, it should be underlined; if typed it should be italicized.

Kit de Waal's coming-of-age novel, My Name is Leon, is a tale of love and loyalty.

Chapter 3

> **Summary**
> - Carol is coping less: she's crying more, and Leon and Jake have begun to sleep at Tina's for multiple consecutive nights.
> - We learn more about Jake's father: he's 39 and Carol is 25. He seems to be avoiding Carol, but Carol is struggling to accept this.
> - Tina seems very **sceptical** *(having doubts / reservations)* about Tony and Carol's relationship, but doesn't explicitly say so.

Analysis

The chapter begins with a list of all the things which make Carol cry, including, '**when Jake makes a lot of noise; when she hasn't got any money; when she comes back from the phone box**'. As readers, we recognise her emotional state is ***deteriorating*** *(getting worse)*.

Jake and Leon are sent to spend more time at Tina's maisonette. The tone used to describe Jake is tender: de Waal describes how '**he makes special whistling noises when he breathes out and he makes his little hands into fists like Muhammed Ali.**' Adjectives such as '**special**' and '**little**' demonstrate the love Leon has for his brother, and the sensory imagery highlights how closely Leon watches his brother.

Carol comes to collect him, and tells Tina that she has tracked down Tony, Jake's father. It becomes clear that she has been trying to get hold of him on the phone, but he's not been answering. Carol manages to track him down at a friend's house: '**I kept on knocking and then he answered the door. Tony did. Just like that.**' Although the reader recognizes that this is unhealthy behaviour, Carol says '**I told you he wasn't avoiding me.**' She reveals that he is living with '**that cow**' and if she finds out about Jake, he won't be allowed to see his daughter any more.

Tina is uncharacteristically quiet: '**Tina isn't asking questions like she usually does.**' When Carol reveals that Tony's told her he's going to move out, she mentions '**At his age, he wants to settle down for good**.' She reveals he is 39, and she is 25. We also get more of a sense of Carol's self-centred nature- Carol claims when Tony leaves his girlfriend, **'it's gonna be just me and him**.' Tina has to prompt her- **'and the kids.'**

One of the key themes of the novel is lies and truth. In this section, the reader can infer that not only is Tony lying to Carol, but Carol is lying to herself about the suitability of their relationship. The final line of the chapter also develops this theme- Leon **'doesn't feel like telling Jake about living with a girl and a cow in Bristol because Jake would probably start to cry.'** The reader understands that it is Leon who wants to cry, but he's *repressing* (keeping in) his feelings and not acknowledging to himself that it is he who is upset. Despite the sadness of this line, there is also an undercurrent of humour- Leon's *naivety* (innocence; lack of experience) means he thinks the '**cow**' is a literal cow, rather than Carol referring to Tony's girlfriend in a ***derogatory*** *(critical / disrespectful)* manner.

Questions

1. Where else in the novel have you seen the theme of lies and truth?
2. Why do you think that Tina doesn't explicitly say anything critical of Tony to Carol?
3. Research Muhammed Ali. Do you think the allusion to him in this chapter is significant?

Terminology

Allusion- A reference to a famous person, setting, event or work. Allusions can be direct or indirect.

List- A number of connected things listed consecutively

Sensory Imagery- Words which evoke any of the senses. Sensory imagery can include:
- Visual Imagery (Sight)
- Auditory Imagery (Sound)
- Olfactory Imagery (Smell)
- Gustatory Imagery (Taste)
- Tactile Imagery (Touch)

Chapter 4

Summary

- The summer is dull. Leon remembers his father threatening the dog next door as he plays with his action men in the garden.
- A man comes to the door, and Leon imagines defending his mum. The man is Tony, Jake's father, and he's asking Carol to stop trying to contact him through the phone or speaking to his friends; their relationship is over.
- When Carol goes to fetch Jake to show Tony, Tony sees Leon and his action men. He pretends to shoot him, but leaves.
- Carol shouts at Leon, blaming him for making Tony leave. Leon is upset and angry, and decides to steal from Carol the next day.
- The next day, Carol is sorry. She reiterates the need for Leon to get a good education so he can **'get out of this shithole'** and **'do better'**. She makes him promise to look after himself and Jake.
- Sometimes Leon goes to school, but sometimes he stays home to look after Jake. Carol is spending more and more time in bed.

Analysis

The chapter starts with a description of the summer: **'the sky is the same colour as the garden slabs, dull and grey.'** De Waal uses pathetic fallacy to emphasise the dullness of Leon's summer.

As Leon sits, he remembers an argument his dad had about the neighbour's dog **'word for word'**- **'If the fucking beast gets into this yard and bites my kid, I'll rip its fucking heart out.'** This moment can be interpreted in a few ways- Byron clearly feels protective towards Leon and wants to look after him, but the fact that he uses profanity aggressively in front of Leon shows that he does not go about his parental responsibilities in a positive way- like Carol, his intentions and love is good, but his methods are flawed. His aggression and violence have evidently influenced Leon as **'Leon imagines its little dog heart beating underneath [its skin] and his dad's hands grabbing Samson's front paws and tearing them apart until the dog howls.'** De Waal's use of graphic imagery disturbs the reader, and we worry that a child so young is imagining such a horrific scene.

Leon continues to play with his Action Men- he dreams of having another two for Christmas, which would make four altogether. The family's financial situation is clearly not good.

The doorbell rings, and Leon and his Action Man '**both crawl on their elbows'** to the door. A man is there, looking like '**the bad guy from James Bond'**, and Leon imagines '**If he has got a gun and he tries to shoot, Leon will kick the door off the hinges and attack him before he can pull the trigger**.' The start of this chapter reminds the reader of the power of a child's imagination.

The reader is further reminded of Leon's age as '**Leon wishes he didn't always need the toilet when he gets excited or frightened. He bunches his trousers at the front and squeezes his crotch into the carpet to stop his wee coming out.'** Later in the text, Maureen often has to remind him to pee before he does anything exciting.

The man is Tony, and he '**speaks slowly with his head on one side like his mum is a baby or she's a bit slow.'** He is clearly *patronising (speaking down to)* her, and Carol is crying as he tells her that he wants her to stop contacting him- he doesn't want a relationship, doesn't want her to keep ringing the house, and visiting his friends.

Carol says he hasn't even seen his child yet, and Tony insults her saying '**You're a proper beautiful bird but you've got a brain like a rusty motor.'** However, as he's speaking his tone shifts: '**Leon and Carol both hear it at the same time. They hear the man's voice go from soft to hard**.' The reader worries he might become violent. However, he again reiterates that he wants her to stop contacting him, and offers her some money.

Carol rushes out of the room to collect Jake, and Tony sees Leon. He makes a friendly and playful gun movement towards Leon after seeing his action man, then leaves. Carol is upset at Leon and screams at him: '**Why are you so f***ing nosy, Leon? Eh? You're always creeping around, listening to things**.' The reader recognises that she's lashing out at Leon, but when they see how upset Leon is and his coping strategies (he counts the triangles on his wall to distract himself), they might find it hard to show sympathy.

De Waal writes, '**Carol used to say sorry when she shouted at him but she forgets all the time these days so tomorrow he's going to take some money out of her purse.**' This is the first we hear about Leon's stealing, but this is a motif that continues throughout the text. Leon seems to steal both as a punishment for those who he sees as doing him wrong, but also as a way to assert control onto an environment that is impossible for him to regulate.

The next morning, Carol apologies, and makes pancakes as a treat (though cries when Leon doesn't like them). She makes Leon make a promise to '**Look after him and look after yourself. Get something more out of life.**' However, she quickly reverts to relying on him to look after Jake. Even when he goes to school, '**Leon has to wake his mum up before he leaves to remind her about Jake. Sometimes she tells him to go away and he spends the whole day thinking about Jake's dinner or Jake's nap-time.**'

At school though, there is some normalcy at times- Leon plays football, and describes showing a new boy around. The new boy has a dog who he claims he's trained to bite people. Leon dreams about him and Jake becoming '**famous for training dogs. The best dog trainers in the world.**'

Questions

1. The theme of dreams and reality is developed in this scene. What dreams does Carol have, and what is her reality? What dreams does Leon have, and what is his reality?
2. Do you think Tony was justified in how he treated Carol?
3. Some ideas about the class system are developed in this chapter. What contrasts can you see between Leon and the new boy, Adam?

Terminology
Graphic Imagery- Something described in shocking detail, often with blood or gore.
Pathetic Fallacy- The weather / environment reflects the emotions of the characters / the atmosphere of the text
Profanity - Swearing

Chapter 5

Summary
- The summer holidays begin, and Carol's mental health is getting increasingly worse. Leon is having to look after Jake every morning now, and develops routines to soothe him.
- There's no money, and Carol has gotten into such a bad state in terms of her mental health that she wets the bed and does nothing. Leon is determined to make Carol well.
- When Leon goes up to ask Tina for some money, she comes down to check on Carol. When she sees the state of the house and children, she calls for an ambulance and social services.
- Jake and Leon stay with Tina for a night. Carol is taken to hospital. The next night, a social worker ('the Zebra') takes Leon and Jake away.

Analysis
The chapter begins with the line '**things get jangled up at home**.' The metaphor '**jangled up**' is an understatement, as Leon has no bedtime, no meals prepared, and has to look after Jake most of the time.

Leon develops routines for looking after Jake, and lists these *meticulously* (thoroughly / in detail). Carol is getting increasingly ill: '**She goes to bed all the time so Leon has to do everything.**' At one point, Leon tasted one of Carol's pills but spat it out. The reader senses that the situation is getting more and more desperate. There is no more money and Leon has run out of nappies for Jake and food for them both. Carol seems to be in a *stupor* (unresponsive state), not moving even when Leon touches her lips. The worst part is when '**He realizes that the whole room smells like Jake's nappy and that his mum has wet the bed again. He opens the window but only a little crack in case Carol gets cold.**' This is a desperately sad moment, as Leon tries to look after his mum with no support.

Leon remembers a time when his mum previously couldn't look after him, and he stayed with a foster family. He didn't enjoy that, so asserts that '**he will look after Carol and Jake, he will make her some tea and toast.**' The anaphoric listing of the imperative 'will' highlights his determination to look after his family. He goes to Tina's to ask for some money, but she insists on coming up to see Carol.

When she comes upstairs, Leon recognises the mess he's left the house is. Tina calls out '**Christ**', and tries to wake Carol up to no avail. She takes Leon, Bobby, and Jake to the phone box to call for an ambulance and social services. She takes the children to her maisonette to wait. When the ambulance comes, the lady talks to Tina. Leon '**wants to tell them that she's kind and nice, but they're not listening.**' In an interview about why she wanted to write *My Name is Leon*, Kit de Waal said that children in care often don't have a voice, and she wanted to write this text from Leon's perspective so that we hear his story from him- not social workers or foster carers. With this quotation, we can see how lost and unheard Leon feels.

The social workers come the next day. They discuss Carol with Tina, and Tina explains how things have been getting worse since they had a '**row**' over Carol borrowing money and not paying it back. We learn that Byron's '**done a runner**' as he '**couldn't face**' court. When Tina asserts that Carol has had a '**proper breakdown**', Leon walks in to interrupt. He says '**Social workers have two pretend faces, Pretend Happy and Pretend Sad.**' Even at this age, Leon recognises that adults lie and hide things from children.

The social worker who Leon calls 'The Zebra' takes him upstairs to get some of his things. She fills a suitcase with some clothes, but '**Leon has to leave one of his Action Men because he has to make some space for Jake's toys and everything won't fit into his red rucksack.**' The rucksack is another motif, as Leon is moved around different homes. The Zebra takes Leon and Jake to a foster lady. He thinks she was '**trying to make him say bad things about his mum.**'

Questions

1. What examples can you see where things in reality are different to how they appear or are *perceived (seen)*?
2. Why do you think Leon's perception of social workers is so negative?

Terminology
Anaphoric Listing- Repeating words / phrases at the start of successive clauses
Imperative- A command verb (in KS2 we call these 'bossy verbs')
Metaphor- Direct Comparison

Chapter 6

Summary

- Leon wakes up in Maureen- the foster lady's- house. She is already awake and playing with Jake, and gives Leon two bacon sandwiches.
- Maureen asks Leon about Jake's routine, and writes it all down for herself. Leon waits for her to ask about him mum, but she doesn't.

Analysis

Leon wakes up, and instinctively realises **'He can't hear Jake crying.'** He remembers that he is at the foster lady's house- he and Jake were dropped off there by the Zebra the night before.

As soon as the foster lady saw him, she kissed him, and let him watch television whilst she spoke to the Zebra. Through snippets of conversation we hear some of the realities of the home situation which were only previously hinted at: **'malnourished... failure to thrive... drug dependency [...] squalor...'** The ellipsis hint that there are other things that are missing. However, midway through a sentence the lady tells the Zebra (who she calls Judy) to leave.

Leon had three biscuits and a hot chocolate before bed, and **'didn't even dream.'** Dreams are another motif in the text, and the fact Leon doesn't dream here suggests he finally feels safe knowing that Jake is being looked after.

The narrative returns to the present. Leon's bedroom is designed for boys his age, and the smells of food lure him downstairs. The lady makes him a bacon sandwich, and is singing a nursery rhyme to Jake. She keeps talking to Jake and telling him words.

As Leon eats his second sandwich, the lady introduces herself as Maureen. She seems to have instinctively grasped what Leon needs, saying **'Not everyone would be able to see the resemblance between you two [...] but Maureen can.'** The house is comforting, and **'smells of sweets and toast and when she stands near the kitchen window with the sun behind her, her fuzzy red hairstyle looks like a flaming halo.'** Already, Leon sees Maureen as a saviour as suggests by the simile used to describe her hair.

De Waal establishes Maureen as an archetypal caregiver- she feeds both boys, looks after them, and makes them feel safe. She is presented as a complete foil to Carol- whereas Carol didn't feed or support the boys' development, Maureen seems (even from this chapter) to selflessly do what is best for both Leon and Jake. This idea is also highlighted by the '**painting of Jesus with all his disciples and he's showing them the blood on his hands**' and the '**giant wooden spoon [which] says "Best Mum"**'. Maureen is presented as a character who is prepared to sacrifice herself for those she loves. This perhaps foreshadows her illness later in the text- she neglects her own health because she's so focussed on Leon's.

After establishing some basics about the boys from Leon ('**He's the boss**') with humour and care, Maureen asks Leon to tell her Jake's routine. She writes everything down (including '**No chewing gum**'), demonstrating how much she understands Leon's psychology- he has been the one responsible for Jake, and here he's symbolically handing the control over.

After the list, Maureen says, '**He wants to say thank you, Leon, love. Thank you for looking after me so well. That's what he'd say if he could speak.**' She acknowledges the role Leon has taken in Jake's life without speaking about his mum or criticising her. The chapter ends with Leon taking a bubble bath, and Maureen listing names of things to Jake.

Questions

1. How do Maureen's interactions with Leon and Jake juxtapose the actions of the other adults we've seen so far in the text?
2. Maureen and Carol are foil characters. List their similarities and differences.
3. List the ways Maureen makes Leon feel comfortable in this chapter.

Terminology
Archetype- An idea, character, symbol or pattern that appears in stories around the world regardless of culture and team. It seems to symbolise something universal about the human experience.
- Caregiver- A character who is selfless and sacrificing, supporting and caring for others.

Ellipsis- Three dots (...) used to show that there are elements to the sentence missing

Foil- A character who serves as a contrast to another character, to highlight particular aspect of their character

Foreshadowing- Hints about what will happen later on the text

Narrative- Story

Essay Hint- Embedding Quotations
Using Square Brackets

Quotations should 'flow' in your analysis; when someone is reading your essay out loud, they should not be able to tell which are the author's words and which are your words. It is the job of quotation marks to reveal this!

❌ 'A flaming halo.' De Waal uses a simile to suggest that Leon sees Maureen as angelic.

✅ De Waal uses the simile 'a flaming halo' to describe Maureen's hair: she is seen by Leon as angelic, or a saviour.

Sometimes, the quotation doesn't properly flow in the sentence. You can use square brackets to change parts of the quotation or miss things out. If you miss out part of the quotation, include a [...].

❌ Maureen is often aligned with images of tenderness and care, such as 'a giant wooden spoon and it says "Best Mum".'

✅ Maureen is often aligned with images of tenderness and care, such as 'a giant wooden spoon [which] says "Best Mum".'

Have a look through the quotations in this chapter. How have they been embedded at different points in the sentence? Where have square brackets been used and why?

Chapter 7

Summary

- Sometimes Leon can't sleep, and Maureen asks him to recount his memories as she says she doesn't see the point of stories.
- Leon tells her about when his dad found out Carol was pregnant with Jake. He was having a dream about leading soldiers, but his dad's swear words kept coming through into his dream. In his dream, he saw himself and comrades dead. He went to the toilet, and heard his father call Carol '**crazy**.'
- The next morning, Carol was singing, but sadly. Her face was red and swollen.
- Maureen promises Leon will have good dreams.

Analysis

Despite everything being happy and calm with routines at Maureen's, '**Sometimes […] Leon can't sleep.**' He goes into Maureen's room and asks for a story, but Maureen says she doesn't see the point of stories- she likes memories, '**Things that really happened.**' The reader recognises that this is her non-intrusive way of finding out about Leon's past.

Leon tells the story of when Byron found out that Carol was pregnant with Jake- another man's child. Leon was dreaming about being a soldier, '**but the words from downstairs kept getting in the way.**' In his dream, Leon is leading his men through a jungle, and Leon was '**in charge.**' However, the shouting kept intruding, '**sliding under the door and flying around the room like angry bats.**' Leon knew that if he stayed asleep, '**he would carry on hearing the words and eventually he would wet the bed**', but if he woke up to go to the toilet he'd have to consciously hear what was being said. The dream continues, but ends dramatically with all his men dead '**And Leon was dead as well and he looked down on his khaki green uniform and his sweaty face from the jungle heat and at the trail of sticky blood that ran out of the corner of his mouth and he stepped over himself and got out of bed.**' After Leon was awake, he went to the toilet but didn't flush for fear of being heard. His dad was calling his mum '**crazy.**'

This dream is important on a few counts. Firstly, it symbolises Leon's protective nature. Even in his dreams, he wants to protect those around him and be seen as brave. However, it also shows how things happening at home affect Leon's psychology- the simile used to describe Bryon's words as being like **'angry bats'** in his room demonstrates that Leon feels unsafe. The ending of the dream is characterised by graphic imagery, which makes the reader feel uncomfortable and worried about what Leon has seen in this past to make him picture death so clearly.

The next day, Leon got up and heard his mum singing. However, when he went downstairs **'the room was full of smoke'** and Carol was **'looking in the mirror, singing with her voice al broken up.'** Her face was **'red on one side and her eyes were puffy and half closed.'** We get the impression that Bryon hit her the previous night.

Leon remembers that **'just because she's singing, it doesn't mean she's happy.'** Again, the theme of appearance verses reality is prominent here- people can pretend to show emotions they're not actually feeling.

Leon drifts off to sleep at the end of the memory, and Maureen promised Leon, **'You'll have lovely dreams tonight, Leon, love. Sssh, lovely dreams. I promise**.' We see the juxtaposition between Leon's life with Carol and Leon's life with Maureen clearly.

Questions

1. Do you believe Maureen's reasons for not liking stories?
2. What other evidence do you have from this chapter for Maureen being a foil character for Carol?
3. Where else have dreams come up in the text? What is the significance of these dreams?

Terminology
Juxtaposition- A contrast between two things
Symbolism- A symbol is where something represents something else in a text.

Chapter 8

> **Summary**
>
> - As it gets closer to Christmas, Maureen starts cooking more and more.
> - Leon thinks because his parents have left, there will be no one to get him or Jake presents. Leon gets angry at the dinner table and cries.
> - The next day, it is Christmas day. Jake and Leon both have lots of presents, including Action Men (for Leon), and Big Red Bear (for Jake).

Analysis

The chapter begins with a list of the food and snacks Maureen cooks for Leon. He's missed out on a lot of nourishment in the past, and it's almost as if she's trying to make up for years of underfeeding. She starts to call Leon '**Pigeon**' and Jake '**His Nibbs**' (slang for a self-important man).

Maureen asks Leon if he's written to Santa, but he gets frustrated because he thinks the parents are the ones to give the presents. He remembers overhearing a conversation about his mother disappearing: '**Legally, it's abandonment.**' As his father skipped bail, he'll be sent to prison if he's caught: '**When they catch up with him, he won't be seeing daylight for a long time.**'

Leon gets upset about this, and pushes his plate away. He redirects his anger onto her: '**Maureen's dinner is sitting in his belly like a bag of sand and he's getting angry with her**.' He begins to cry, and explains that he doesn't care about his presents and he knows Santa doesn't exist. Maureen asks if they should tell Jake he doesn't have presents, and Leon protests that he has bought Jake the baby drums. Maureen reminds Leon that both she and the social worker would have bought Jake something. Maureen is cleverly alleviated Leon's concerns about not getting presents without actually addressing the issue directly, as Leon claimed he didn't care about the presents.

The next morning, Leon goes downstairs and there are more presents than he was expecting. 'Jake' has got him an action man, and Maureen has bought him an action man with a jeep, alongside other presents. Maureen bought Jake '**Big Red Bear',** an important motif for later in the text, and Maureen herself received cookbooks (again, a <u>symbol</u> of her archetypal caregiver role). Leon is delighted, and hugs Maureen: '"Steady, pigeon," she says but she hugs him back and kisses his cheek. "Merry Christmas, Leon, love."'

Questions

1. What evidence is there from this chapter that Maureen really understands Leon's needs?
2. Why is Leon's love for Action Men significant?
3. Later in the novel, Leon often steals, particularly when he's angry or frustrated. What hints do we have of this tendency in this chapter?

Terminology
<u>Slang-</u> Informal language

Essay Hint- Embedding Quotations
Speech within a quotation

There are two options for quotation marks- 'single' or "double". You can use either, as long as you keep it consistent in your essay!

When you are including a quotation from the text with speech marks, you can use the other form.

If you've been using single quotation marks for your quotations:

✅ *Leon is delighted, and hugs Maureen: '"Steady, pigeon," she says but she hugs him back and kisses his cheek. "Merry Christmas, Leon, love."'*

If you've been using double quotation marks for your quotations:

✅ *Leon is delighted, and hugs Maureen: "'Steady, pigeon,' she says but she hugs him back and kisses his cheek. 'Merry Christmas, Leon, love.'"*

Chapter 9

Summary

- Leon and Jake have been living with Maureen for six months. Leon thinks he has a groove on his 'neck back' from Maureen pushing him there.
- Leon cuddles Jake as he sleeps, and thinks about how much he loves him.
- Leon knows someone is coming to the house as things have been tidied away. Salma, a social worker Leon calls Sally, came earlier in the week to bounce Jake.
- The social worker tells Leon that Jake is going to be adopted. Maureen gives Leon a Curly Wurly.

Analysis

Leon thinks that the **'little dent'** between his skull and spine is from Maureen pushing him- not hard, but often- when she asks him to do things. Leon calls this his **'neck-back'** because he thinks that is what his father would have called it. He remembers how Byron used **'funny words'**, like saying **'soon come'** when he left the house. However, **'That's when Leon's mum used to get annoyed with him because he never came soon and he never came back when he said he would. And now she's doing the same thing.'** Leon recognises the *hypocrisy* (claiming to have higher standards than someone else) of this situation, and clearly feels betrayed.

Leon is holding Jake, and watching Jake breathing through his **'tiny perfect nostrils'**. Maureen picks up Jake, and moves them downstairs. Leon realises everything has been packed away, and notes: **'Someone is coming. Leon knows who it is. The air is different.'** He reveals that 'Sally' (actually called Salma) has been coming to visit, saying Jake **'has to have a chance'** and looking at Leon in a sad, but **'not pretend sad'** way. Maureen has been **'quiet for days'**, and keeps looking at Leon and saying **'It's a bad, bad, world.'** We also hear that she calls Social Services a **'waste of bloody space'** when she's on the phone to her sister, Sylvia. Through de Waal's use of <u>limited third person point-of-view</u>, the reader is only seeing what Leon sees and knows, and it therefore builds <u>tension</u> and <u>anticipation</u> in the reader as we wonder what is going to happen.

Salma arrives, and begins talking to Leon, and '**Leon agrees with everything Salma says**' although he clearly doesn't understand the true implications. Salma reveals that Jake is going to be adopted by a new family. She claims Jake will send Leon letters, and Leon reminds her that '**Jake can't write.**' Salma laughs and says his new family will write for him.

Maureen dismisses Salma curtly, and takes Leon to get a Curly Wurly. Leon is surprised as it's not Saturday or Christmas, and his bedroom is a mess. Leon is excited that there are three other Curly Wurlys in the drawer, but the reader recognises this means hard times to come.

Later that night, Leon asks Maureen '**What's adopted?**' Maureen explains, and when Leon asks why she says: '**Because, love. Just because. Because he's a baby, a white baby. And you're not. Apparently. Because people are horrible and because life isn't fair, pigeon.**' This is one of the first hints we see of racism in the novel- as a biracial older child, Leon is less likely to be adopted than his white baby brother. Maureen says Leon can stay with her.

 *Look at the Concepts and Contexts page on **Racial Tensions** to understand more about attitudes towards race.*

Questions

1. In this chapter, we hear some of Maureen's views on social workers. How does she react differently to what she feels? Are there any moments where we can see her true emotions coming out?
2. Why do you think Leon said he understood what Salma was saying when he didn't really?

Terminology
Anticipation- The expectation of something big happening, or a climax occurring
Tension- Building conflict for the characters

Chapter 10

Summary

- Half term comes and Jake still hasn't been taken by a family.
- However, one day Maureen picks Leon up by herself and lets Leon have some chewing gum.
- A few days later, Maureen tells Leon that Jake has been chosen by a family to adopt.
- Leon has a meltdown, throwing the biscuit tin and trashing the room whilst singing.
- Maureen comes up and doesn't tell him off about the mess; she just asks him to come down for tea.
- When Leon says no, she picks up biscuits which have been thrown on the floor, and places them next to a new photo of Leon and Jake and Big Red Bear. They go down for ice cream.

Analysis

It gets to half term, and Jake is still with Maureen and Leon. However, one day Maureen picks Leon up from school without Jake. When Maureen says it's '**Great**' that Salma and a '**nice lady and her husband are looking after him**', '**Leon knows she's pretending.**' Although Leon is very young, he can clearly sense when the adults around him are lying or trying to disguise their emotions.

Maureen treats Leon differently on the way home- she holds his hand even though '**she hasn't done that for ages**', and gives Leon some chewing gum. When they return home, Salma is alone with Jake and nods to Maureen, and '**It was a nod that puts Maureen in a bad mood for the rest of the day.**' As readers, we can guess that the lady and her husband have decided to adopt Jake.

The next day, Maureen reveals the news to Leon that the family are picking up Jake today. She rocks Leon and hugs him, but Leon asks the question he's been avoiding because he knew the answer but did not want to hear it said aloud: '**Am I going with him?**' Maureen is almost crying as she tells Leon he will be staying with her. This is an incredibly poignant moment in the text- de Waal has established Leon's love and devotion for Jake from the very first chapter of the novel and reiterated it throughout, and the reader feels sad and upset that Leon and Jake are going to be separated.

De Waal is raising questions here about the ethics of social care and separating siblings- even now, almost 40% of siblings are split up when they're taken into care.[1]

 *Look at the Concepts and Contexts page on **Social Care** (in Cultural References, Page 115) to understand more.*

When the lady and husband come to collect Jake, '**The lady doesn't look at Leon, she only looks at Jake, and her blue eyes are sparkly and bright as well because she's trying not to cry like Maureen**.' Leon is upset: his '**trousers are too tight and he wants a wee and his legs feel bendy and he's very angry with Maureen.**' The use of polysyndeton emphasises Leon's excess of emotions- he doesn't know what to feel, and feels a range of overwhelming and conflicting emotions all at once. As the handover is completed, Leon goes into the kitchen to take the biscuit tin, throws the plain biscuits over the fence, and puts the chocolate digestives into his pocket. Leon refuses to say goodbye, and storms up to his room.

Leon slams the biscuits on his dresser. He hums and sings music- *The Dukes of Hazzard* theme song and Jake's baby programmes- and throws his clothes and mattress on the floor, and '**He piles a blanket over his head and sits on the mess he's made and he sings until he lets out every word and all the space comes back into his chest and his belly, until he isn't angry with Maureen so that when she opens his door he doesn't want to hit her**.' Here, he has clearly understood the significance of what has happened, and doesn't know how to cope with his overwhelming emotions.

When Maureen enters, she doesn't comment on the mess, but asks if Leon is coming down to tea. She starts to pick up a few things in the room, and Leon sees a new photo of himself and Jake next to Big Red Bear on his bedside cabinet. She '**kisses him on top of his head, which**

---

[1] https://www.childrenscommissioner.gov.uk/resource/siblings-in-care/#:~:text=An%20estimated%2037%25%20of%20children,accommodation%20are%20separated%20from%20siblings.

she has only done once before when he had a nightmare about drowning', and says that they can skip tea and go straight to ice cream.

Questions

1. How does Maureen try to cope with this difficult situation? How is this different to how Leon and Carol cope with their difficult situations?
2. What makes this such a moving moment in the text?
3. Do you think separating Leon and Jake was the right thing to do? Why, or why not?

Terminology
<u>Polysyndeton-</u> A list using multiple conjunctions (connectives)

Essay Hint- Writing about character

A key thing which separates a lower level essay from a higher level essay is being able to step outside the text- you need to write about the characters knowing that they are constructs of the author made for a purpose, rather than real life characters. **Look at these excerpts from essays- how does the second essay write different about character?**

❌ Leon is angry when Jake is taken away. He goes up to his room and has a tantrum, ending up 'sit[ting] on the mess he's made and [singing] until he lets out every word.' He struggles to deal with his difficult emotions, and is so overwhelmed he can't act rationally. This is a sad moment; the system is not fair.

✓ <u>De Waal demonstrates</u> Leon's anger when Jake is taken away, <u>describing him</u> going to his room and having a tantrum, ending with him 'sit[ting] on the mess he's made and [singing] until he lets out every word.' <u>Perhaps de Waal wanted to explore how difficult it is for children</u> to deal with difficult emotions; they can get so overwhelmed they can't act rationally. <u>The reader feels sadness for Leon, but also their own anger about the unfair system.</u>

Chapter 11

> **Summary**
>
> - Maureen wakes Leon up from a bad dream as he's been grinding his teeth. She makes him have a wee, have some orange juice and a biscuit, before talking to him on the sofa.
> - She makes him count how many children she's looked after- 30 including him- as proof she knows about children.
> - She promises Leon he will be alright, and he will see Jake again.

Analysis

The chapter begins with Maureen waking Leon up from a dream about fighting a dragon because Leon had been grinding his teeth. Teeth grinding is often linked to stress and anxiety[2], and the reader realises that Leon's mental anguish at Jake leaving is affecting him physically as well. In the dream, Leon was about to defeat a dragon who had been terrorising people- again, his dream symbolises his desire to protect others.

Maureen makes him have a wee, despite his tiredness, and takes him downstairs to talk. He eats a biscuit, and Maureen says '**I know you're upset but you and me are having words**.' She makes him count up all the children she's looked after- 22 fostered, 2 biological children, 3 grandchildren, 2 stepchildren, and Leon- number 30. She uses this as evidence that she knows a lot about children, and tells Leon: '"**You will be all right, Leon. You will be all right.' Leon uses the tea towel again because it's better for tears. 'And one day,' she says, 'you will see your brother again.**'" She admits that it may not be for a while, but says '**I'll keep saying it until you believe me, Leon. You will be all right and that, mister, is a promise**.' She reassures him he'll be okay.

> **Questions**
>
>
>
> 1. Maureen has no way of knowing for sure Leon will be okay, or that he'll see Jake again. Is it okay for her to lie like this?
> 2. What else does Maureen do to reassure Leon this chapter?

---

[2] https://www.nhs.uk/conditions/teeth-grinding/

Chapter 12

Summary

- Salma arrives, and Leon eavesdrops. Maureen is still angry that Leon and Jake have been separated.
- Leon steals some money from Salma's purse. Maureen shuts the door so he can't listen anymore.
- He reads his mum's file from Salma's purse. We learn Carol had an '*itinerant lifestyle'* *(travelling often with no permanent home, usually due to poverty and homelessness)* and 'emotionally unstable personality disorder.' She is dependent on alcohol and prescription drugs, and isn't capable of looking after her children.
- Leon walks into the kitchen and asks when he'll see his mum. He gets given a biscuit.
- He goes out, messes up Salma's bag, and dribbles biscuit in it to punish Salma.

Analysis

Salma arrives, and Leon eavesdrops: **'He crouches down, and if they're not whispering, he can hear what they say.'** We learn that Leon does this lots- one time, Maureen said **'Margaret Thatcher could kiss her arse and Leon laughed and got caught earwigging.'** This is one of the many times that we hear <u>allusions</u> to politics in the novel, although ideas about Margaret Thatcher are never fully explored.

 *Look at the Concepts and Contexts page on **Cultural References** (Page 115) to understand more about Margaret Thatcher.*

Leon goes downstairs to eavesdrop more, and knows they're talking about him. Maureen and Salma are discussing his school report- he doesn't have any friends and won't do work, despite being intelligent. Maureen says **'He's grieving if you ask me.'** Salma reassures her they've done the right thing to give them both a chance, but Maureen **'snorts'** and interrupts: **'Jake's got a chance, you mean. You've split them up and in my books that's a sin and I won't change my mind on that**.' We learn how emphatically Maureen disagrees with the choice to split the brothers up.

As they continue talking about the **'good match'** Jake and his new family have made, Leon steals a 50p coin from Salma's purse (50p is about the same as £2.75 today). Maureen checks on Leon, and then goes back to Salma and closes the door. De Waal describes how '**Leon dashes upstairs faster than a cheetah. He slips the fifty pence under his mattress. He'll move it later. He comes downstairs so quickly and so lightly that he's out of breath again.**' The simile, fast pace and frantic tone show much of a big deal this is for Leon- he has taken money out of Carol's purse for food, and snuck extra biscuits, but has never taken this much money before that we know of.

He comes back down, and takes one of the files from Salma's bag about his mum. The reader gets more information about Carol- she has an '*itinerant lifestyle*' *(she moves around a lot)*, has '**an emotionally unstable personality disorder**' which is '**complicated by her dependence of prescription drugs and alcohol use.**' She has a '**high level of self-interest as opposed to the interests of her children**'. She's '**failed to attend appointments [and] access visits.**' After reading this, Leon goes into the kitchen and asks '**When am I going to see my mum?**' Salma tries to *hedge* (avoid answering directly) her response, but Leon says he's hungry. Maureen gives him some biscuits and sends him away.

In the living room, '**he sits down by the papers that say horrible things about his mum. [...] He stands over the mess and dribbles the soggy biscuit from his mouth on to the papers, a brown sticky mess with crumbs in it.**' We can see that he's punishing Salma for the things she's been saying.

Questions

1. We get hints in this chapter that Leon is not making good behaviour choices- he's stealing, not trying in school, and punishing people. Do you think he's justified in his actions?
2. Why do you think that Carol hasn't taken up the opportunities to see her sons?
3. Why do you think Leon steals?

Terminology
Pace- Speed of the sentences

Chapter 13

Summary

- Leon hears a train. He's never been on a train before. He thinks in the future he'll find his mum by using a train. He hears the birds, and reflects on the fact Jake used to be really noisy- everything seems to remind him of his family.
- Maureen is getting up later and later without Jake. She says it's because of her **'chest'**, Leon thinks it's because there's no reason to get up without Jake.
- Leon knows he'll get angry if he thinks about Jake leaving, so he eats lots of food.
- Maureen decides that they will go on a bus ride to see her sister, Sylvia. They have to take the bus to get there, and then walk up a steep hill. Maureen clearly struggles going up the hill.
- When Maureen gets to Sylvia's house, she can't breathe. She says she has a **'tight chest'**, and Sylvia blames her **'wheezing'** on her sugar intake.
- Maureen and Sylvia start reminiscing and looking over old photographs.
- When they think Leon isn't listening, they start discussing him. Leon goes to the toilet, but on his way back he locks the back door and steals the key.
- Sylvia makes Maureen promise to go to the doctors. Sylvia threatens that she'll make Leon sorry if she doesn't remind her to do it.
- The next morning, Maureen is still ill. Leon takes her up coffee and toast, but she's looking and sounding very unwell.

Analysis

The chapter begins with a series of mini time shifts. Leon hears a train, and imagines that '**One day, he's going to get on a train and find his mum.**' He hears birds, and remembers how '**sometimes Leon would make bird noises for Jake, and Jake would pull Leon's lips like he was trying to grab the sound before it come out.**' He says, '**Sometimes, thinking about Jake makes Leon feel sick.**' In this opening, we see the power of memory- everything in the present makes Leon remember his family.

Maureen is still in bed- she's staying in later and later and claiming it's because of her '**chest',** but Leon thinks '**the reason Maureen is still in bed is because there is nothing to get up for**.' Of course, at the end of this chapter we realise the fragility of Maureen's health, but Leon believes that without Jake no one would want to get up.

Leon believes '**The empty sound in the house is louder than Jake crying for his bottle.**' When grieving, the absence of a loved one is painful, and this metaphor describes that feeling perfectly. Leon struggles to manage his emotions: '**if Leon turns round and looks at Jake's cot in the corner of the room, he knows that he will get angry with Maureen so he picks at a scratch in the wallpaper and puts the pieces in his mouth. They taste of fish fingers.**'

Leon gets up and eats a lot of breakfast. Maureen says that they need something to do on the '**miserable Saturday',** and says they'll go to see her sister, Sylvia. On the way, Leon doesn't want people think that Maureen is his mum as '**she's fat and her hair is too orange.**'

When the reach the bottom of the hill leading to Sylvia's house, we see more signs of Maureen's declining health: '**She tells Leon to carry her shopping bag and she shuffles along the pavement with one hand on her chest and the other swinging in the air. She has the same face as when she cries and Leon hopes she won't start until she gets where they're going.**'

When they get to Sylvia's house, Maureen is struggling to breathe so much that Sylvia thinks something has happened. Leon doesn't like Sylvia- he's only met her once at Christmas and Sylvia didn't speak to him- and when Sylvia '**turns suddenly to Leon and points the cigarette at him**' and asks him what happened Maureen has to defend him, saying '**She's not blaming you.'** Maureen explains '**Got a tight chest, that's all. Got a sort of wheezing rattle or something every time I try and do anything.**'

Leon plays with his action men whilst Sylvia and Maureen talk, mostly about memories of their past. They *reminisce (remember with pleasure)* about '**the olden days',** and there is a stark juxtaposition between Leon's painful memories at the start of the chapter, and these gossipy musings.

After a while, their conversation turns to '**whispering'** and they talk about Leon, Jake, and Carol. Leon looks around the house. Leon eavesdrops the conversation, and Sylvia asks, '**That one will get adopted, won't he, what's his name again?**' Maureen replies, '**Leon. Not a chance. That's what they say.**' Leon locks the back door, and pockets the key. We see him again punishing people for what they say about him and his family.

As they leave, Sylvia makes Maureen swear to go to the doctor. Maureen says '**I swear, yes. Leon will remind me, won't you, love?**' Sylvia replies, in a threatening tone, '**You make bloody sure. If you don't and anything happens to her, you'll be sorry.**'

Initially, this threat seems harsh, but the next day Maureen is so ill she can't get out of bed. Although Maureen tries to reassure Leon about her health, '**Leon can hear the crackling sound that comes from her throat like a cough that won't come out. And her face was the same colour as the sheets. He can tell when Maureen's trying to be happy and when she's worried and he knows now why Sylvia kept making her promise.**' The chapter ends with an uneasy sense of foreboding.

Questions

1. What are your initial perceptions of the character of Sylvia?
2. There are several moments in this chapter which explore ideas about memory. Compare Leon's memories with Sylvia and Maureen's memories. What do you notice?
3. What ways does Leon find of dealing with his painful emotions in this chapter?

Terminology
Foreboding- A sense that something bad will happen.

Chapter 14

Summary

- Maureen has been talking about Leon's mum on the phone: she's been **'in and out of institutions.'** Maureen is critical of her, saying **'I'd have to be pretty sick to keep me from my kids.'**
- It's been a year since Leon has been living with Maureen, and his mum is coming to visit him.
- A sports car drops Carol off, driven by her new boyfriend. Carol has bought Leon a pen and pencil set. Leon notices how she's changed- her fingers and skin have a yellow tinge and she's emaciated.
- Carol is upset that Jake has been adopted. Maureen keeps trying to get Carol to think about Leon, but she doesn't.
- We learn the new boyfriend is called Alan. Carol says she wants to change her behaviours.
- Maureen gets Leon to show Carol his bedroom. She tries to hug him but pulls away. She crumples to the floor when she sees the photo of Jake.
- Carol asks for the photo, but Maureen says no. She explains how hard it's been for Leon, and how he's turning **'light-fingered'**.
- Leon gives Carol the photo of Jake as she leaves.
- Later that night, Leon clutches his bear and worries about when his mother will return, and lots of questions about her and Jake. He says all the 'bad words' he's been holding in.

Analysis

This chapter starts with Maureen using **'her no-nonsense voice'**. She's been on the phone, **'saying bad things about [Leon's] mother. Again.'** It turns out social services have been in contact, and Leon's mother has been sick, in and out of various **'institutions'** **'up north, then Bristol and God knows where else.'** Maureen is very critical of Carol, saying **'I'd have to be pretty sick to keep me from my kids, know what I mean?'**

Leon is frustrated, as he feels like Maureen doesn't know Carol. He's now nearly as tall as Maureen. Maureen makes him wash his hands, and says he's going to have a visitor. It's revealed Carol has said she'll visit before, but always not turned up, so Maureen kept it quiet this time.

Leon notes that '**Maureen often says nice things and nasty things both at the same time.**' Again, the theme of deception and pretending in front of children comes up.

Maureen warns Leon that his mum may be different to how he remembers her. A sports car turns up, and the driver is a man who Leon doesn't know. There is a long wait, and then the man walks Carol to the door, and **'Carol is smiling but she's crying as well.'** She crumples to the floor, but the man catches her. She says she wants to go on her own. Maureen welcomes her in.

They sit on the sofa, and Carol asks how Leon is without looking at him. She is trying to find her cigarettes: '**She always does this and Leon has to take the bag and look for her. He tries to take the bag off her but she snatches it away and he sees Maureen frown**.' Leon immediately reverts back to his protective role, but Carol seems to not remember. Despite this, he sits close to her '**because he belongs to her and she belongs to him.**' Ideas about family bonds and biological families are highlighted. Carol has bought Leon a gift- a pencil and pen in a wooden box, that **'looks like it belongs to a teacher or a professor.'** There is a stark contrast between the age-appropriate presents Maureen buys for Leon, and we are reminded of how both women are foils for one another.

Leon notices the differences is his mum: '**her teeth and fingers are yellowy brown like mustard and her cheeks go in like a skeleton.**' We can see that Carol hasn't been looking after herself, and recognise the necessity of Leon being looked after by Maureen. However, the reader might also feel concern that Carol evidently hasn't been getting any support for her psychological problems. Carol struggles to hold the coffee Maureen brings her, and says '**I was so ill I couldn't tell you my own name.'**

In one of Kit de Waal's other books, *Supporting Cast,* she writes about small moments from different characters' lives. One of the short stories is about a moment when Carol had a breakdown in Bristol, trying to find Tony.

See the chapter on Biographical Context to learn more about Supporting Cast.

Carol explains more about what has been happening in her life, and how she's spend time in The Maybird Centre, which seems to be a sort of halfway house. She then mentions Jake, and breaks down: "**'They took my baby,' she says and starts to cry again so that her coffee shakes in the cup. 'My baby.' Maureen puts her hand on Carol's and squeezes. 'Leon took it very badly too, Carol,' says Maureen**." The juxtaposition between these characters is clear- Carol thinks primarily about herself, whereas Maureen thinks about Leon.

Maureen tries to turn the conversation back to Leon, but Carol zones out and seems to be muttering to herself silently. Carol then starts speaking about Alan, the man in the car: **'It was the best day of my life when I found Alan.'** She says how he wants to take them all to the seaside, but Leon **'doesn't want to share his mum all the time.'** Carol says she can visit more, but only when Alan gives her a lift because the bus makes her ill, and **'Leon sees Maureen raise an eyebrow and fold her arms.'** Maureen is clearly critical of Carol.

Leon takes Carol up to see his room, and she praises its neatness. She says **'I do remember, you know, Leon. I remember you taking care of me.'** She touches her forehead to Leon's, and it's a tender moment, **'but then suddenly she draws back and takes a deep breath.'** She looks around his room, and seems to be showing interest in Leon's life, but then **'She catches sight of the picture of Jake on the white carpet and crumples down on his bedroom floor.'** Leon fetches Maureen to help him, and they get her to the bed and she continues to cry. Maureen's tone changes as she tells Carol **'You're frightening him.'** Carol calms down a bit, and they go downstairs.

Carol asks for the photo of Jake, but Maureen says: **'Er, no, Carol. No, you cannot. That picture was taken by me for Leon. Paid for by me. He hasn't got much else, has he? He's not at home with you where he should be and he hasn't got his brother, which he's finding bloody hard if you don't mind me saying.'** She goes on a *tirade (long rant)* about how hard Carol's illness has been for Leon, and how he's falling behind at school, has no friends, and is stealing. Carol ignore this, and starts to get ready to leave.

Leon holds her hand, and **'She squeezes his fingers and he can feel her love travelling all the way down from her heart into his. It's like special electricity, a secret**.' The <u>figurative language</u> used in this moment is touching and tender, and again reminds the reader of the bond between mother and child. Leon thinks about what his mother used to smell like, listing all the things he could remember from his old house. However, **'all he can smell now is Maureen's air freshener, stronger than the smell of his mum and where he used to live.'** His memories of home seem to be being taking over by his life at Maureen's.

Maureen tries to speak to Carol, reminding her what a lovely son she has. Carol ignores her, and reassures Leon that Alan is looking after her. As the car pulls up, Leon runs up to get the photograph of Jake. He gives it to his mum. She calls him a **'little angel'**, and drives off without looking back. As she leaves, Leon **'feels a dark star of pain in his throat and the last warmth of her touch on his fingers.'** This chapter highlights to the reader Carol's selfish and self-absorbed nature. She thinks primarily about herself and her suffering, and seems unable to comprehend Leon's pain.

Maureen tries to speak to Leon, saying he's **'a bloody good kid considering.'** She tries to hug him, but Leon pushes away, angry that she doesn't seem to like his mum. Leon **'knows what his mother knows. That someone else is holding Jake and kissing him. Someone else is looking into the perfect blue of his perfect eyes. Someone else is smelling him and touching the soft skin on the back of his hand.'**

At the end of the chapter, Leon misses the photograph and holds onto Big Red Bear. He says **'all the bad words he has stored up all day since his mother came and took the photograph and drove away without him.'**

Questions

1. Do you think we're supposed to feel sympathy for Carol in this chapter, or not?
2. What other ways is Maureen a foil character to Carol?

Terminology
Contrast- Something opposing / opposite
Figurative Language- Anything that's not literal, such as similes and metaphors

Chapter 15

> **Summary**
>
> - Leon has to call the ambulance for Maureen, who wakes up sweating and rasping.
> - At the hospital, Leon has to explain his home circumstances which upset him, but he cheers up when the policewoman is kind and buys him hot chocolate and a doughnut.
> - Sylvia comes into the hospital, and in contrast to her previous attitude towards Leon, she's now thankful and appreciative of him for saving Maureen's life.
> - From snippets of dialogue, we learn Maureen had bronchial pneumonia with complications and will not be out of hospital for weeks. Sylvia offers to look after Leon.

Analysis
The chapter begins with an ambulance arriving: Maureen has woken up struggling to breathe, and Leon had to call 999 for her. He waits for the ambulance to arrive and leads them up to Maureen's room, and '**Leon decides he might be an ambulance driver when he grows up.**' Maureen wants to hold his hand, '**but he's scared to touch her in case she dies. This might be the time that there's no one to look after him.**'

At the hospital, Leon is looked after by a policewoman who asks him lots of questions about Carol and Jake. He cries, and the policewoman reassures him that Maureen won't die. She calls him '**a brave hero and a clever boy**', and manages to get him to cheer up by getting him a doughnut, hot chocolate, and letting him press the buttons in the police car and play with the walkie talkie. Leon thinks '**The policewoman is a bit like the nurse at the hospital when Jake was born: when she says something you believe her**.' Ideas about trust and honesty are explored.

As Leon is watching a gangster film on the TV, Sylvia '**bursts into the room.**' In contrast to her previously dismissive attitude in Chapter 13, here she is grateful to Leon, saying '**You saved her life,** chick. Good boy, good boy. Thank you.' She kisses him, although Leon doesn't like her old lady smell.

Later, an emergency social worker comes, and talks to a doctor, the policewoman, and Sylvia. Through snippets of <u>dialogue</u>, we hear that Maureen has **'bronchial pneumonia with complications',** and will be weeks in the hospital.

Sylvia says that she will take Leon: **'He's a good lad. He's saved her bloody life, he has. She always said he was a good kid, Mo did. I'll have him. Yes, I will. Bless him**.' It's agreed that Sylvia will take Leon to Maureen's house and look after him there; she's been a registered carer so they know she has the checks necessary. The social worker reassures him that **'we will try to keep you at home. I think you've had a pretty rough time lately and we don't want to add to that, do we?'**

Questions

1. Kit de Waal has worked for family law, sits in on adoption panels, and writes training manuals on adoption and social care. How do you think this has influenced her in the writing of this chapter?
2. Why do you think Sylvia agreed to look after Leon?
3. What hints are there that this is going to be a turning point in Leon's life?

Terminology
<u>Dialogue-</u> Speech

Essay Hint- Introductions

Sometimes, the hardest thing about writing essays is beginning. If you have a set introductory sentence starter, which you know you can use for whatever essay, it can alleviate 'blank page anxiety.'

In Kit de Waal's 2017 coming-of-age novel, <u>My Name is Leon</u>, ideas about ___ are presented through…

Chapter 16

Summary

- The chapter begins with a list of things Leon doesn't like about living in Sylvia's house.
- Leon tells the Zebra he wants to find his mum and move in with her, but we learn Carol is in a halfway house in Bristol.
- Leon is upset that he can't live with his mum, and that he's not allowed to see Maureen.
- The social worker brings him a gift- a BMX.
- There's a big shift in <u>tone</u> and <u>pace</u> when Leon is on his bike- he enjoys the freedom and speed of it as he rides. He sees a black man on a bike with yellow sunglasses who he thinks looks like a wasp, and admires him.
- The Zebra offers to take him to visit Maureen the next week if she's better.

Analysis

Leon starts a list of things he doesn't like, and the first three are **'Sylvia. Sylvia's house. Having to move to Sylvia's house even though they said he could stay at Maureen's house but they lied.'** Other things he hates include **'People pretending all the time'**, and lots about not being allowed to talk about Jake. This list reveals some of Leon's frustrations and anxieties.

The social worker Leon calls The Zebra comes to speak to him, and explains that he can't live with his mum as she's in a **halfway house** *(a house for rehabilitating patients)* and needs to prove she can look after herself and her children before anything happens. Although Leon is frustrated by the Zebra and dislikes her black and white stripey hair, **'out of all the social workers he's ever had, she looks at him the most.'** We see Leon's need to be seen and heard.

Leon lists some of the things he does to stop himself getting upset or angry, including picking scabs, playing with things, or stealing. Leon is frustrated that he can't look after his mum, like he used to, and that he can't see Maureen. The Zebra says "**Because that's not** being a child, Leon. You're a young boy and your mum is an adult and she has to look after you. Not the other way round. When she can't look after you, we make sure there is somebody else that can. And right now that person is Sylvia.'

The Zebra then takes him outside, and pulls a BLX out of her boot for Leon. She warns Leon to be careful, **'But Leon doesn't want to be careful. He wants to ride as fast as a car. Faster than a car. Fast as a rocket.'** This string of childish similes reminds us of Leon's youth- despite everything he's been through, he's only 9, a little boy. He cycles and feels exhilarated. The bike seems to be a <u>symbol</u> of freedom and independence- with the bike, Leon is free to go where he wants and he can forget about his past as he cycles.

When he's cycling, he sees a black man on a bike who looks **'like a wasp.'** Leon clearly admires the man, describing how **'he turns the corner in one sweet and beautiful moment. Gone.'** We remember that Leon has no adult male role models- he's been looked after by Carol, Maureen, and Sylvia.

When Leon returns to the Zebra, he thinks that **'She's the best social worker in the world.'** She promises to take Leon to see Carol the next week if she's better.

Questions
1. Are Leon's methods of coping with upsetting or frustrating emotions healthy?
2. What have Leon's experiences with social workers been like so far?
3. Do you think Sylvia was right to move Leon to her house?

Chapter 17

Summary

- Sylvia is watching a game show, and Leon asks if he can ride on his bike. He tries to remember the way Wasp Man went.
- He cycles down an ethnically diverse street, and wonders at the array of produce on sale. There are people of many ethnicities: Indian, African, Black.
- He cycles to Rookery Road allotments, and sees an old man hacking down a bush with a big knife.
- Wasp man cycles past, and the old man shouts that he can't cycle in the allotments. Leon follows him in.
- Leon looks at him admiringly, and the Wasp Man fixes his bike for him.
- The old man (Mr Devlin) tells Wasp Man (Mr Burrows) off for Leon being unaccompanied and on a bike. Mr Devlin is Irish, and Mr Burrows mocks his accent and makes faces behind his back.
- Mr Burrows gets Leon a Cream Soda, and starts to teach him about plants. He explains everyone calls him Tufty (because of his baldness), apart from his mum who called him Linwood.
- Tufty explains the sun is a healer, and Leon remembers a good memory of his mother.
- Leon sees that there are many people in the allotment of all ethnicities.
- On his way back, he sees Mr Devlin. He asks about his knife (the Kanetsune), but Mr Devlin refuses to answer any more questions.

Analysis

Leon asks to go for a cycle, and thinks that people are looking at him and admiring his new bike. He thinks how '**He looks big for his age, twelve or thirteen, and now, with his new bike, he could even be fourteen.**'

He cycles in the direction he thinks Wasp Man went, and notices that '**there are loads more black people than where Sylvia lives**.' There are Pakistani men, Indian men, and black men and women. This area of Birmingham is clearly culturally diverse. Kit de Waal grew up in 1980s Birmingham; her mother was Irish, and her father was black in a time where biracial children were unusual. It is nice that this chapter celebrates the diversity of the city.

> *See the chapter on Biographical Context to learn more about Kit de Waal's life and how this may have influenced the text.*

Coming to a crossroads, Leon sees a sign for 'Rookery Wood Allotments' and admires the rows of flowers. He sees an old man swinging a large curved knife, and hacking down a bush. Suddenly, a bike whooshes by- it's the Wasp Man, who calls out **'Easy, Star!'** The man with the knife is angry, and points to the sign saying **'No cycling.'**

Leon follows Wasp Man, and stares at him in admiration. He describes how **'his skin is brown [...] like his dad's but shiny and muscly like the Hulk. [...] He's a warrior.'** The tone is one of admiration, and the comparisons to a **'warrior'** and the **'Hulk'** demonstrate how Leon immediately sees him as someone to respect.

When the man asks if Leon is lost, Leon explains that he too has a bike. Wasp Man examines it, and tightens up some bits with a screwdriver. Leon tests it, but Wasp Man shouts at him to get off as the old man approaches.

The old man is Irish, and Wasp Man greets him with a **'Top of the morning to you, sir.'** Although not racist, the Wasp Man seems to be mocking the Irish Man with a stereotype, and later in the exchange says he doesn't understand the man's accent. There was a very negative prejudice about Irish people in 1980s England, fuelled by political tensions regarding the IRA and immigration. We can see some of these negative views explored here.

> *See the chapter on Attitudes towards the Irish to learn more about how the Irish culture was perceived and mistreated.*

There is significant tension between the two man. The old man **'pointing the tip of [his] knife at Leon'** says **'Children aren't allowed.'** The knife is described in detail- **'Where the knife has been chopping at the hedge there are streaks of green on the sharp blade like alien's** blood.' Leon doesn't seem to recognise the danger of the situation as '**The man raises the knife and points the tip at Leon's neck.**'

The old man- who is named Mr Devlin- is on the allotment committee, and explains that the '**regulations**' are important. The black man is called Mr Burrows, and mimics Devlin's accent. Tension builds, and **the men look at each other like they're about to start fighting,**' but Devlin walks away and Burrows '**makes a monkey face behind his back just the way Leon does when Sylvia tells him off.**' Burrows criticises how Devlin '**thinks he owns this place.**' As Devlin retreats, Leon notices how he looks strong.

Mr Burrows invites Leon (who he calls '**Star**') for a drink. Inside the shed, Leon picks up a box of dominos and remembers a set his father had. Burrows takes them off him and says it's a '**Big man's game.**' Dominoes are a common Caribbean game, often played loudly and rambunctiously between older Caribbean men.

As Leon looks around the shed, he notices some plants- '**The silver-green leaves are so thin and delicate that he can see threads of tiny veins like the veins on Jake's hands**.' Leon is interested about the plants, and Mr Burrows seems to be a natural teacher: '**Mangetout. Say it. [...] Means "eat all"**'. He gives Leon a Cream Soda, and explains his name is Tufty- people call him that ironically as he has no hair. His mum calls him Linwood, and only Mr Devlin calls him Mr Burrows.

As they sit down in the sun, Tufty says '**The sun [...] is a healer. When the sun comes out everybody smiles. World looks different. You can manage in the sun what you can't manage in the rain.**' This reminds Leon of a time when he went for a walk with his mum in the rain; she'd forgotten the cover for Jake's pram and everyone was upset when they got home. He remembers how later that night, she said '**You're such a good boy, Leon. I'm sorry if I'm not the best mum. I love you, you know.**' Leon thinks '**That's what sunshine feels like.**' It's poignant that this moment- one which shows Carol's inability to care for her children- is one that Leon remembers as being full of 'sunlight.'

Leon looks around the allotment, and sees people in saris, turbans, and an array of clothes. He realises how huge the allotments are. He thinks that '**There are no swings or slides but it's better than a park because everybody has their own bit of land to look after and they can do what they like with it.**' Again, Leon wants to look after people and things.

As Leon heads out of the allotment, he sees Devlin, who tells him off about the bike again. Leon asks what the knife is called, and Devlin explains it's a **'Kanetsune'**- a traditional Japanese knife. Leon follows him to his hut, and wonders if it's a halfway house. The chapter ends with him cycling back.

Questions

1. From the first chapter, we've been told how Leon is big for his age. Do you think that his size affects how people speak to him and expect him to behave?
2. What signs of prejudice can you see between Tufty and Devlin?
3. Nicknames are important in the novel. Make a list of all the nicknames characters have for each other. What do they reveal?

Essay Hint- Tentative Language

When writing an essay, we do not know why the author did particular things. We need to be **tentative** *(cautious and exploratory)* when we discuss the text. Using adverbs of possibility like 'perhaps', modal verbs such as 'could' and 'may', and considering alternative explanations can make your answer sound more thoughtful.

De Waal's references to sunshine in this chapter could symbolise hope- she may be using this image to make the reader consider how hope and happiness help people to 'heal' and 'manage.' Alternatively, sunshine might instead represent contentment: in the allotment with his plants, Tufty is happy; with his mother being loved, Leon is happy.

Chapter 18

Summary

- Leon recounts how Sylvia collects her pay and buys Leon a comic and a doughnut every week.
- When he's falling asleep, he tells her a tale about how he used to grow mangetout with his parents and chop down trees. He's clearly making it up from his time at the allotments.
- Leon used to watch programmes on weekends after lunch, but now he likes to cycle to the allotments to talk to Tufty.
- He doesn't tell Sylvia where he's going, and Sylvia tells him to speak to a policeman if he's lost, then retracts that, telling him to ask a lady instead.
- Tufty gets Leon to read out some seed packets, and they plant the seeds together. Tufty gives Leon some 'take a chance' seeds.
- After watching Tufty, Leon goes to Mr Devlin's allotment. Mr Devlin shows him how to oil the knife. He tells him his name is just Devlin, and he used to be called Senor Victor, or Papa. He disappears into his shed.

Analysis

Some of Leon's routine is described. On Saturdays, he watches TV shows before they go to the shop Sylvia works in to collect her pay. We see briefly how the shop owner asserts authority over her ('**He holds on to [her pay] until she tugs it away with a fake smile and when they get outside she calls him a bastard.**' On the way back, she buys a magazine for herself and a doughnut and comic for Leon.

As Sylvia puts him to bed, Leon tells a story about how his parents had a huge garden: '**My dad gave me a sharp knife and I used to help him.**' It is clear that Leon is *assimilating* (*combining*) his real life with fantasies of how his life could have been.

On Saturday afternoons, Leon always asks to go out on the bike. He takes things like pictures or football cards to show Tufty. Sylvia is a little bit suspicious, and makes Leon show her his left and right. She says '**If you get lost, ask a policeman. Second thoughts, if you get lost, ask a lady, any lady.**' This is one of the first hints we've had about tensions between the black community and policemen. Police in 80s Birmingham were granted powers such as being able to stop and search anyone who looked suspicious (sus laws), and there was a lot of tension as black people were being unfairly stopped. It's sad that institutionalised racism and the discrimination of black people by the police is something still familiar to a modern reader.

> *See the chapter on Racial Tensions to learn more about Sus laws and prejudice in 1980s Birmingham.*

When Leon gets to the allotments, the day is beautiful. Leon sees Tufty, and reads out to seed packet to him. Tufty invites Leon into his shed: **'Come in [...] You'll learn something.'** Inside, there are pictures of black men on the walls, and some of the images have 'Black Power' written underneath them.

The **'one in a suit and tie with a moustache'** could be an allusion to Martin Luther King, a human rights activist in the US.

The **'man with his fist in the air and a medal around his neck'** could be an <u>allusion</u> to the 1968 Olympics Black Power Salute. Tommie Smith and John Carlos (both American) won medals for the 200 metre race. On the podium, they raised a black gloved fist in the air for the national anthem. They wore no shoes but black socks to represent black poverty.

Leon **emulates** *(copies)* the man in the poster, and makes a fist in the air- the sign of Black Power. Tufty makes a comment about the man being brave, but then turns back to teaching Leon about growing plants- he tips some seeds into Leon's hand, and tells him to plant them. This moment could be **emblematic** *(illustrative)* of Tufty's desire to not fight- he wants to live in peace. He calls them **'Take-a-Chance seeds'**, as you don't know what will grow. Tufty gives Leon some of these seeds, and Leon tucks them away in his pocket. He teaches Leon that plants need soil (a **'blanket'**), **'food in their belly'** and **'drink'**- by personifying the plants as humans who need to be looked after, the reader can see why Leon feels such an **affinity** *(connection)* with growing plants- he likes to look after people.

On his way out of the shed, Leon pockets a 10p piece. He watches Tufty for a while, and then cycles to the allotment gate where he sees Mr

Devlin. Devlin has his blade, but won't let Leon touch it as it's dangerous. Leon sees some seeds, and recites what he's learnt by reading Tufty's seed packets. Leon sees another knife which Devlin says needs oiling, so Devlin sits down to show him. The blade is sharp, and as Devlin '**holds Leon's hand and draws the stem of the flower all along the edge of the blade'**, it cuts the flower. Devlin describes it as '**Beautiful […] Imagine the damage it does.'** The reader might feel a sense of concern about the fascination Devlin has with the blade.

Devlin cuts a piece of T shirt for Leon to oil the handle of the knife, and Leon is impressed. As Leon oils the handle, Devlin asks Leon his name. He introduces himself as '**Leon Rycroft. And I have a brother.'** Leon's identity is connected to Jake. When Leon says Mr Devlin's name, Devlin says '**Just Devlin. I used to be Señor Victor. Can you say Senhor Victor**?' After Leon repeats this, '**Mr Devlin stares at Leon and then whispers, "Or Papa."**' He sighs as Leon repeats the word 'Papa.' This is, again, a slightly disturbing moment for the reader, and they may wonder what Devlin's intentions are with Leon.

Leon finds out more about Devlin's background- he's from Ireland, but hasn't been back in 20 years. Devlin tells him off as he wipes the knife on his jeans, saying Leon's mother will be angry, and Leon doesn't explain about his foster family. Suddenly, after both criticising and praising Leon for his cleaning of the knife, he goes into his hut. Leon waits for a while, then cycles home.

Questions

1. In what ways are Devlin and Tufty similar? In what way are they different?
2. Why do you think Tufty is spending time with Leon? Why do you think Devlin is spending time with Leon?
3. There are more and more hints in this chapter of racial discrimination and political tensions. Why do you think de Waal has included these subtly, through snippets of dialogue and allusions?

Chapter 19

Summary

- Leon goes to visit Maureen in hospital with the Zebra.
- Maureen asks how Leon is getting on, and Leon complains about his bedtime and the curtains in his bedroom.
- A nurse assumes Maureen is Leon's nana, and he realises how old she really is.
- Leon thinks about how the adults in his life keep repeating the same things: Don't worry, he can't see Jake, and Carol isn't well.

Analysis

The Zebra keeps her promise, and takes Leon to see Maureen in hospital. Leon notes that '**She smells different, she looks different and she sounds different but when she snuggles him and rubs his back she is the same.**' This will be a familiar feeling for many readers who may have visited loved ones in hospital.

The Zebra goes down to the café, and Maureen asks questions about her and Sylvia. Leon notes that '**Her mouth is smiling but her eyes are sad.**' In a book where adults frequently lie to Leon, it is interesting that he can see through her false expression.

Leon talks more and more to Maureen, asking why she can't come back, and telling him about the allotments. She drifts off to sleep, and a nurse calls Maureen his nana: '**Leon looks at Maureen and realizes she is very, very old. She has lots of white in her hair now and soon she will look like the other old ladies and soon she will die**.' As the nurse tries to take him to the Zebra, he knows what she will say as adults only ever seem to say the same things: '[**Don't worry. [...] He can't see Jake. [...] Carol isn't well.**' We can see how frustrated Leon is with the many elements in his life he can't change, and how inefficient the phrase '**Don't worry**' is when he has so many things to worry about.

Questions

1. Leon knows that Maureen is pretending to be happy when she's smiling. What other moments in the text does he seem wise beyond his years?

Chapter 20

Summary

- Leon tries to visit the allotments every day. Today, Tufty is there with some friends (Castro, Marvo, Waxy, Stump and Mr Johnson) playing dominos.
- Castro is angry that Mr Johnson is 'turning the other cheek', but Mr Johnson explains they have to organise to seek reform. They're talking about black rights.
- Castro thinks they have to form an army rather than a lobby group to be listened to. The others seem to disagree with both Mr Johnson and Castro.
- Tufty shows Leon some of the seeds growing, whilst the others argue. Mr Johnson walks off.
- Tufty reads out a poem he calls 'conspiracy.' The poem is about how he breaks up with his girlfriend, but his mum makes him work so hard he goes back to her. Castro criticises him for only thinking about girls, and storms off.

Analysis

Leon always goes to the allotments when he's on his bike, to see Devlin, Tufty, or even others there (like Mr and Mrs Atwal, the Indian couple).

One day, Tufty is there with his friends playing dominoes, while old Mr Johnson watches. They are playing dominoes vigorously and talking in fast West Indian accents.

Tufty introduces Leon to the men as 'Star'. He says his friends are called Castro, Marvo, Waxy, Stump, and Mr Johnson. Mr Johnson is the only one to not have a nickname- perhaps a sign of respect. Castro's name could <u>allude</u> to Fidel Castro- a revolutionary communist leader who ruled Cuba. He was a controversial leader- many people admired how he fought for Cuban Independence and against the Imperialism of America, but he did rule as a dictator. Out of Tufty's friends, Castro is the one who wants to create an **'army'**, so we can see why this name might be <u>aptronymic</u>.

When Mr Johnson leaves for a church meeting, Castro gets angry, and accuses him of **'turning the other cheek.'** Mr Johnson tells Castro, **'you don't have the monopoly on anger, on a sense of injustice.'** He claims that **'we have to organise [...] form ourselves into a body which society recognises, that can lobby the authorities and seek redress.'** Evidently, Mr Johnson and Castro both have the same beliefs but want to use different methods of achieving them. Castro says **'If we come together to form something, it's an army. [...] You think white people going to listen to monkeys? Monkeys is what they call we.'**

The men all begin to argue, and it seems that no one agrees totally with either Castro or Mr Johnson. Tufty keeps out of the argument, cleaning up and providing drinks, before showing showing Leon how the seeds he planted have started to grow. Tufty calls them **'babies. [...] Fragile. Babies need looking after.'** He lets Leon plant them, and shows how they need bamboo sticks for support.

When they come back, the argument seems to have reached a climax. Castro references the stop and search laws (see page 108), and won't let Mr Johnson speak. He ends by telling Castro to **'Don't bite the hand that feeds you [...] Work with the hands God gave you**.' He walks away.

Tufty changes the topic by reading the group a poem he wrote called 'Conspiracy', about how a girlfriend and his mum conspired to get Tufty to go back to the girl. It's funny, and breaks the tension, but Castro doesn't laugh. He accuses Tufty of only thinking about girls, and walks off.

Questions
1. Names are important. What other names in the text do you think are significant, and why?
2. De Waal is much more explicit about racial tensions in this chapter. Why do you think this is?
3. What do you think works better to instigate change- violent or peaceful protests? Why?

Terminology
Aptronymic- A name which suits the characters' characteristics.

Chapter 21

> **Summary**
>
> - Leon doesn't like his new school. He doesn't have many friends, although he sometimes sits with Martin, another child who is in foster care. Martin sometimes fights.
> - Sylvia has to go in for a meeting about Leon's behaviour. He hasn't been trying, has been swearing, and always asks to go to the toilet. Sylvia explains on the way home about remote controls for the TV. Leon wishes he has a remote for the TV so he can turn Sylvia, social workers, and teachers off.

Analysis

The chapter begins with a list of things Leon hates about his new school. Despite many people (Tufty, Maureen) commenting on how good a reader Leon is, his teachers insist he needs to **'catch up.'** This could be a comment on the failings of the education system to support those in foster care or who move schools sufficiently. Leon's only friend is another child in foster care- Martin- who often gets into fights.

Sylvia is called in for a meeting about Leon's behaviour. Leon notes how **'Teachers are like social workers, with lots of different pretend voices and smiles.'** Again, Leon picks up on the insincerities of adults. The teachers tell him off for swearing, asking to go to the toilet, and not making effort. When Sylvia backs them up, Leon recognises by a glance the teachers make that they don't like Sylvia.

On the way home, Sylvia stops by a television shops and says about a new invention- a remote control. Leon fantasises about this: **'If Leon had a remote control he would lie in bed and turn Sylvia off, click, and the teachers off, click, and the social workers off, click, click, click. Then he would crush the remote control with a big hammer so they could never come on again.'** We see his frustrations.

> **Questions**
>
> 1. What seems to be the main difference between the adults Leon admires and those he doesn't?

Chapter 22

> **Summary**
>
> - It's half term. As Leon cycles, he imagines he can fly and see Jake.
> - At Sylvia's, Sylvia has lots of women around. They are planning a party for the wedding of Charles and Diana. Sylvia makes a list of jobs for everyone. Leon steals the list and hides it in his pencil case.
> - Watching the news that night, there is a piece about Carpenter Road- a road nearby. There are emergency services and a smell of burning.
> - Leon goes in and steals some money from Sylvia's purse.
> - There is a riot on Carpenter Road.

Analysis

It's half term. Leon goes to the allotment but no one is around, so he cycles quickly and imagines he's so fast he's flying, and can see Jake. When he gets home, there are lots of Sylvia's friends around. Leon is disappointed as it's not Maureen, and he's upset as everyone keeps telling him Maureen will be home soon but they're lying. The women are planning a party, and Sylvia makes a list of what everyone can contribute. It turns out, they're planning to have a street party to celebrate the marriage of Diana and Charles. Leon steals the list.

Leon is allowed to stay up late watching television as it's half term. However, Carpenter Road- a road near them- is on TV. They go outside, and see emergency service vehicles going down the street, and **'There is the smell of a bonfire in the air, and a hushed, excited feeling.'** As Sylvia is distracted outside, Leon goes into Sylvia's purse. He imagines stealing the ten-pound note and having enough money to find his mum, Jake, and then buy some cream sodas for Tufty. However, he puts it back and takes 40 pence instead.

He goes back out to Sylvia, who explains **'They're running around breaking windows and robbing.'** The reader recognises that there has been a riot.

> **Questions**
>
> 1. Do we have any more sympathy for Leon's thievery in this chapter?

Chapter 23

Summary

- Leon has a new batman t-shirt and trainers. He gets Sylvia to cut the bottom off his jeans so he can have cut off denim shorts like Tufty.
- Sylvia asks about his friends from the park. Leon doesn't answer.
- On the way to the allotment, Leon stops in the paper shop and buys a Curly Wurly and some Toffos. The window has been smashed, and he's had to board it up. He asks Leon 'Why are you doing this?', implicitly blaming Leon as he's black.
- When he gets to the allotment, Mr Devlin has been drinking. Leon helps him plant some seeds as he rambles.
- Tufty has a new boom box. They listen to King Tubby's dub, then other dub music.
- As Leon cycles home, he pedals to the beat of dub. He imagines Jake banging his baby drum in time to the music, and he thinks about it all the way home.

Analysis

Leon has a new batman t shirt and white trainers. He debates whether or not to wear them to the allotment, as he knows they'll get dirty but he wants to show them off. He manages to convince Sylvia to let him cut the bottom of jeans to make shorts, as then he'll look more like Tufty. Leon admires himself in the mirror, and decides **'he looks really old, maybe even fifteen.'** Sylvia asks about the friends he's meeting, as Leon has been saying he's hanging around with boys at the park. It seems that Leon knows that Sylvia would disapprove of him being with Tufty and Devlin at the allotment.

Leon has the forty pence he stole from Sylvia, so he goes to the paper shop to buy some sweets. The old Pakistani man sometimes follows him around, and asks for the money before he gives him the sweets. This time, the shopkeeper points out his smashed window and asks **'Why are you doing this?'** The <u>direct address</u> 'you' demonstrates that the shopkeeper is stereotyping Leon as a rioter, just because he is black. Leon doesn't understand this, and goes off to the allotment.

When Leon arrives at the allotment, he sees Mr Devlin, who **'sways side** to side.' Leon can smell whiskey on his breath. Leon helps Devlin plant seeds, whilst Devlin appears to be talking to himself. He appears to be talking about a boy- **'He had so much energy, just like me when I was a boy.'** The reader can infer he is talking about the son he mentioned previously, who used to call him 'Papa.' As Leon helps him water the plants, **'he sounds like a child'** and **'his face is sad and his lips are thin.'**

Leon then goes to Tufty's shed, and the <u>atmosphere</u> here is a complete <u>contrast</u>. Tufty is playing reggae music on his boombox. The batteries have just died, and when Tufty replaces them **'the bass hits Leon like a train'** and **'it's as heavy as concrete.'** The music certainly has a strong influence on both Tufty and Leon, as Leon **'feels his arms rise up all on their own and his feet start shuffling on the wooden floor.'** Perhaps de Waal is making a comment here on the power of music, and how it can be a positive a healing thing. As Leon listens, he imagines chanting 'Black Power' to the beat.

On the way home, Leon peddles to the beat of dub. He wonders what Jake is doing, and imagines him banging his baby drums to the music.

Questions

1. Both Devlin and Tufty have been ***ostrasised*** *(exluded)* from society: Tufty, because of his race; Devlin, because of his Irish background and something mysterious that has happened in his past. How do they both cope with their positions in society?
2. Leon (don't forget he's 9!) is allowed a lot more freedom than children today might be given. Do you think this is a good or a bad thing? Why?

Terminology
<u>Direct Address-</u> Speaking to someone personally with the pronoun 'you'

Chapter 24

Summary

- The Zebra picks up Leon to go to the Family Centre to see Carol, and speaks to Sylvia about Maureen's frailty. They are looking for a permanent placement for Leon.
- On the way to the Centre, there is news about the Riots and Irish hunger strikes.
- When they get to the centre, the Zebra brings up Leon's lying, stealing, and lack of effort at school. She admits it's hard for him.
- At the Family Centre, Carol is clearly ill. She's **emaciated** *(extremely skinny)*, and her eyes are sad. She talks to Leon a bit about himself, and then the conversation turns to Jake. She gets frustrated and starts hitting her head against the wall. Leon acts like Jake to calm her down, and says he can pretend to be Jake any time she wants.

Analysis

Leon goes to the Family Centre to see his mum. When the Zebra picked him up, he overheard her and Sylvia talking about how Maureen would need to be careful when she comes out. The reader recognises it might be doubtful she's well enough to look after Leon as **'We're looking at a permanent plan for Leon.'** Sylvia starts talking about the Royal Wedding instead. The Zebra seems cynical about how much everything has cost, but Sylvia is still excited.

In the car, the news details some of the things happening: **'The wedding and then the riots and the Irishman that starved himself to death, then the Pope who got shot.'** Interestingly, this is all important Political news, but to Leon (as a child), it is background information- he doesn't care about this, so we don't hear much about it. This is the first we as readers have heard explicitly about the 1981 Hunger Strike, but it reminds a reader (particularly an adult reader who may have lived through these events) about why people in England were prejudiced against the Irish.

> *See the chapter on Attitudes towards the Irish to learn more about the 1981 Hunger Strike.*

When they arrive at the Family Centre, the Zebra explains that **'things have got a bit out of hand recently.'** She referencing his lying and stealing, and his attitude at school. She reminds Leon of a promise he

53

made to behave and stop stealing, and Leon references things that weren't in his promise- Jake is with a new family, and he can't see his mum when he asks to. The Zebra recognises it's **'f***ing hard'**, slipping into profanity.

The Zebra has picked up Carol from 2 hours away, and warns Leon she might be tired and that she's still not well. The Zebra talks to another social worker- Bob- who explains that Carol's been wandering around frustrated that it's taking so long.

When they enter the room, Carol is playing with a doll. When Leon enters **'she turns slowly and smiles but she's not really looking at him.'** Leon recognises how skinny she has gotten and how her eyes look **'like she's never been happy her whole life.'** She hugs Leon, but Leon **'feels a fresh worry for his mum because no one is looking after her.'** Again, Leon's caring and protective nature is coming out. After hearing about his negative qualities from the Zebra earlier in the chapter, we are reminded of why Leon is like he is.

Carol starts smoking, and the Zebra asks her to do it by the window. Carol ignores her. Leon takes some of the papers he was told to bring out of his bag, like his school report. When Carol asks him if he's clever, Leon **'looks at the Zebra'** who replies that he is. Carol takes a long time to read the report, and Leon gets frustrated at her slow reading speed. She hints for the Zebra to leave, asking **'Is this a supervised visit?'** and the Zebra leaves. Carol says she **'looks like a f***ing badger'**, and both Leon and Carol start laughing hysterically. However, the funny moment turns sour when Carol starts acting like a dog on the floor and trying to tickle Leon. He then **'holds her hand still and she rests her head on his knees.'** Symbolically, this is a reversal of the typical maternal image we expect to see of a child leaning on a mother's lap, and demonstrates how the roles have reversed in their relationship.

After the Zebra checks on them, the conversation turns to Jake. Carol and Leon exchange memories of him, and Leon shows Carol Big Red Bear. When Leon asks Carol if she still has the photo of Jake, Carol is non-committal, and **'she leans against the windowsill and starts knocking her head on the glass.'** Leon starts to speak and act like Jake to calm her down, and she holds him and cries. Leon says **'I could be him, mum. [...] You could come back for me and, sometimes, I could**

be him.' This is a poignant and devastatingly sad moment- Leon seems to recognise that Carol cares for Jake more than him, and tries to find a solution to make Carol feel better.

Questions

1. What evidence is there in this chapter that Carol is selfish and unable to consider the needs of others?
2. What evidence do we have in this chapter of Leon's caring and selfless nature?
3. Carol and Leon say that the Zebra is '**not nice.**' Do you agree? Why, or why not?
4. Compare this to Chapter 14 when Carol visits Leon at Maureen's house. What signs are there of her deteriorating mental and physical state?

Essay Hint- Assessment Objectives

Before you write your essay, it's important to know what you're being assessed on and how to get the marks. You should be familiar with the mark scheme before attempting an essay, but below the key success criteria for each Assessment Objective has been summarised.

AO1- Understanding of text and task
- Have you fully answered the question, looking at **WHAT** the author explores about the character / theme?
- Have you backed up your ideas with references to the text?

AO2- Writer's methods and effects
- Have you zoomed in on **HOW** the writer has created ideas about theme or character?
- Have you used subject terminology, such as character, theme, symbol, setting, atmosphere, and structure?

AO3- Contexts and Concepts
- Have you zoomed out to **WHY** the writer has created these ideas, considering the context of the time and wider ideas?

AO4- Technical Accuracy
- Have you written your response using correct spelling, punctuation, and grammar?

Chapter 25

Summary

- Leon wakes up thirsty from a nightmare about ogres and giants. He has a fever- probably the flu.
- When Leon asks Sylvia for a story, she tells him a joke about a rabbit. Leon thinks he's been tricked. He goes back to sleep.
- The next morning, Leon is still poorly. He imagines being strong like a superhero.
- He remembers his mum and the fact he's left his bed and toys behind. He gets angry, but looking at his stolen items makes him feel calmer.
- He remembers how his mum didn't say goodbye to him at the Family Centre.
- The next morning, he is slightly better, and is allowed to go to the allotments.

Analysis

Leon has a bad dream that an ogre is cooking him, and then he's running across a desert away from a giant, and he's thirsty. Sylvia wakes him up, and it turns out it was a fever dream and Leon is poorly. Sylvia gives him some water and tablets. She says **'says you've got to be twelve on the packet but you're about the size of a twelve-year-old. Can't hurt.'** Leon cries and struggles to take the tablets, and opens the window to cool him. She fans him with a comic, and Leon admits **'Sylvia isn't as nice as Maureen but she is cleverer.'**

Leon asks for a story, and Sylvia thinks for a while. She tells him a long joke with the climax being a <u>pun</u> about hare-restorer and hair-restorer. However, Leon thinks **'it isn't a story, it's a trick.'** Again, he feels deceived by adults. Sylvia says **'We all have adventures, some are good and some are not so good'**. She recognises that Leon is in the not good phase. Sylvia makes him go to sleep.

In the morning, he's still feeling poorly. He remembers that Maureen told him to stop having bad dreams he needs to think about nice things, so he thinks about presents and the Incredible Hulk. He imagines he is the Hulk, and **'no one can stop him doing anything. He thinks about being strong and having powers like Superman or Batman and then**

he feels Sylvia covering him up with a blanket.' Leon's *perceptions (views)* of strength are quite naïve- he associates strength with physical strength and being in control, not recognising emotional strength and resilience as important.

As Leon drifts into sleep, he remembers him mum tucking him under a blanket when she and Byron were at the park with him, and when he woke up he was in his own bed at night. He wonders who is in that bed now, and remembers the toys he left behind. He gets angry and throws off the covers.

Returning to his room, he gets his red rucksack. This seems to be a symbol of constancy and control- Leon has taken it to all of the homes we've seen him in, and it has come with him on his visit to see his mum. He looks inside at **'all the things he's collected'** (a euphemism for stolen) and feels better. It seems that looking at what he's stolen gives him a sense of calm and control, when there are so many other things in his life he can't control. He remembers saying goodbye to his mum at the family centre, but **'he doesn't see her turn around and wave because she didn't.'** This is another heart-breaking moment.

The next day, Sylvia allows Leon to stay off school again as he's still hot, despite having more on an appetite. Leon uses this time to cycle to allotments.

Questions
1. How does this dream differ to Leon's other dreams?
2. Compare the ways Sylvia deals with Leon asks her to tell stories to the way Maureen deals with the same request (Chapter 7). What do you notice?
3. Sylvia comments that Leon looks like a 12-year-old, despite the fact he's only 9. Does she treat him like a 9-year-old? Does he act like a 9-year-old? Why?

Terminology
Pun- A joke with a play on words
Euphemism- A more polite way of saying something rude, controversial, or upsetting

Chapter 26

Summary

- There aren't many people at the allotments. Leon cycles to the end, and finds an old shed.
- On his way back, Leon waters Tufty's plants but thinks he hears Jake. He spins around looking for him, and faints.
- He wakes up in Devlin's shed. As Devlin goes to fetch his bike, he looks around. There are lots of interesting items, but also lots of photographs of boys.
- When Devlin comes back, Leon asks if a pistol he's spotted is real. Devlin doesn't answer, and as Leon cycles back he thinks about how much he wants to visit the shed again.

Analysis

There aren't many people at the allotments. Leon cycles past lots of things on the **'scruffy land that no one wants'**, and ends up at an old shed. It's noted how **'nobody looks after this shed. Nobody wants it'** (a <u>metaphor</u> for Leon himself?). He decides **'it's perfect.'**

On the way back, Leon stops to water Tufty's plants. However, he suddenly has a **'funny feeling. Something reminds him of Jake and he straightens up quickly as though he can hear him cry.'** He stands up and looks around, hoping to spot his brother. He keeps turning, and feels **'the full feeling in his chest and the pounding of all the questions that nobody answers and then all Tufty's plants float up past his eyes like wisps of dancing, fluttery green feathers.'** He has fainted in the heat because of his illness.

He wakes up in Devlin's shed, and Devlin gives him some water and tells him to go home. However, as **'Leon sits up straight […] his legs are empty and weak'**, and Devlin tells him not to go yet, his voice **'soft like Maureen's.'** We can see his *paternal (fatherly)* side coming out. Leon is concerned about his bike, so Devlin goes to collect it.

Leon looks around the shed. There are lots of unusual items- a bow and arrow, an old toy train, a gas mask, a posh teapot, and a wooden spear with a carved head. Leon notes that **'everything is old but nothing is**

dirty.' These are evidently cherished possessions from Devlin's past with significant sentimental value.

However, behind the items are **'photographs of boys, lots of them; dozens.'** One boy features prominently in many. The reader feels significantly uncomfortable at this moment, remembering that Leon is a vulnerable child in the shed of a man with unknown motives. However, Leon gets distracted though by the weapons- a knife, and a **'real pistol.'**

When Devlin returns, Leon is standing by the knives, and Devlin doesn't answer. The chapter ends on a slightly sinister note, as Leon notes **'there are things in Mr Devlin's shed that he wants to see again.'**

Questions

1. Look closely at the items in Devlin's shed. What can the reader infer about him based on these items?
2. Who do you think the boy that appears in many of the photographs is?
3. What might Leon want the shed for?

Essay Hint- Planning

If you don't plan your response, you'll struggle for it to get above level 2 ('Supported, relevant'). For the passing grades your essay needs to be 'Explained, structured' (Level 3), 'Clear understanding' (Level 4), 'Thoughtful, developed consideration' (Level 5), or 'Convincing, critical analysis and exploration' (Level 6).

Reading the question, annotating the question, and exploring exactly what it wants you to explore is key. You should then do a brain dump / mind map, before organising your thinking into clear sections to represent each paragraph.

Planning should take you 10 minutes, giving you 30 minutes to write and 10 minutes to proof read and check through.

Chapter 27

Summary

- Leon stays off school because of his illness, but helps Sylvia with chores and shopping for the Royal Wedding celebrations.
- At the allotment, policemen arrive. Leon originally thinks they're for him as he's been stealing, but they go to talk to Castro and Tufty.
- They're looking for Rainbow, who it turns out led the protest which turned into a riot on Carpenter Avenue.
- They're being highly provocative and insulting, trampling over plants and ruining Tufty's shed. Tufty tries to remain calm, but Castro reacts. He gets arrested and dragged away.
- Tufty is angry, and tells Leon to stand up for himself. He implies peaceful protest never works.
- At home, Sylvia is drunk, and tells him a rude bedtime story.

Analysis

Leon has the whole week off school because of his illness. During his time at home, Sylvia makes him help with the chores in the house. They go shopping to stock up on dry goods for the Royal Wedding street party, which is only six weeks away.

However, he just wants to go to the allotment to make improvements to his shed. He has taken some things from Sylvia's house to fix it up, but he needs other things like **'a padlock because Mr Devlin has a padlock and they do things properly.'** Despite the fact that Devlin and Tufty are very different characters, Leon clearly admires them both. Sylvia is suspicious of Leon leaving with a full backpack, but lets him go.

When he gets to the allotments, Castro is there with Tufty. However, a group of men enter, and **'walk straight towards him and they look angry.'** Leon thinks it's the police, after him because he has stolen lots of things- he believes Sylvia has warned them about him and they've come to arrest him. Everyone in the allotment is watching, and they are being careless and trampling over all the plants. Leon **'wishes he was the Incredible Hulk and he could fight them all and run away'**. However, the men walk past him **'and surround Tufty and Castro.'**

The police speak to Tufty, and say '**Long time no see. Never took you for a Percy Thrower**' (a famous gardener on BBC *Gardener's World*. They start looking in his shed, and throwing things around. However, when they address Castro he insults the police, saying '**You blood-clat, Babylon! You beast boys can't come in here for we. You don't have nothing on we.**' Here, Castro is using Jamaican idiolect and slang. The phrase '**blood-clat**' is a Jamaican swear word, an offensive term relating to female menstruation; 'Babylon' is a term used to describe anywhere black people are oppressed; and 'beast' is slang for policemen.

It turns out that the police are not there for Castro or Tufty; they want a man called '**Rainbow**.' The main policeman mimics Castro's slang, saying '**He's your mate, isn't he? Your "brethren", your "spar", your "idrin". That's the lingo, isn't it**.' This is a form of mockery. The policeman then pushes Castro and calls him '**my little carrot head.**' He's purposefully antagonising Castro by using negative language towards his hair colour (he has ginger hair), and being patronising.

Tufty holds Castro back and tells him to '**Leave it.**' However, the policeman carries on his ***tirade*** (rant) of insults, saying Tufty '**Does as he's told**' like his father, and '**Perhaps your balls haven't dropped yet, is that it?**' The policeman is humiliating Tufty for being calm and non-violent, perhaps as a way of trying to incite violence. He calls Rainbow '**that s**t-stirring-windbag-with-the-tea-cosy-on-his-head, Darius White.**' Again, the policeman is mocking the Jamaican culture, by calling the rastacap a tea cosy.

There are five policemen, all in plain clothes. It turns out, they want Rainbow for leading the riot on Carpenter Road, '**chanting and spear-chucking and war-dancing.**' Again, the police are being prejudice against the black men and stereotyping them negatively. The protesters had posters saying '**Down Babylon.**' The policeman say he learnt to write in prison.

Castro retaliates, spitting and saying '**Rainbow speaks for all of we.**' Mr Devlin gestures for Leon to come to him, before fighting breaks out. The policeman manage to grab Castro, and arrest him for '**resisting arrest.**' He fights as he the four policemen drag him out: '**Spit comes out of Castro's mouth like he's a wild dog**', and '**His jeans are pulled** down to his ankles and DC Green is smiling all the time and tightening the belt on his trousers.' It seems like he enjoys seeing Castro humiliated and restrained. As the police are dragging him, Tufty shouts '**Leave him! He can't breathe!**' This is a poignant reminder to the modern audience of the devastating murders of Eric Garner and George Floyd, who after telling policemen 'I can't breathe' were suffocated to death. It reminds the reader that systemic racism still exists in the world, and things still haven't completely improved since the 80s. Black people are still oppressed and victims of police brutality, and systemic racism does exist in some institutions.

DC Green asks Tufty where Rainbow is again. Tufty goes into his shed and takes a shovel, and '**holds it like a sword right up into DC Green's face then slams it into the ground. [...] It judders back and forth and then stands dead straight.**' Tufty says, '**This is my land. [...] My piece of the earth. My f***ing land.**' This small act of defiance causes DC Green to '**laugh so loud that all the fat on his tummy wobbles.**' He kicks the spade over, and says '**Spades don't scare me, Linwood. Not one bit.**' Finally, he leaves, whistling and kicking a stone.

Everything is silent in the allotments for a while, until Tufty shuts at Mr Devlin that he didn't invite them. Most people go back to their gardening, but Devlin looks around the devastation and destruction left by the policemen. He says '**They're the same all over the world. [...] Small minds, big feet.**'

Leon thinks that he's '**been told over and over always to ask a policeman for help but these policemen didn't even have uniforms on and they didn't give Castro a chance.**' Even at his age, he can recognise the unfairness of the situation. He feels betrayed that the very people who are supposed to look after people are insulting them, provoking them, and attacking them.

Leon goes into Tufty's shed, and it's a mess. All of the plants have been thrown on the floor, and the posters ripped up and discarded. Tufty picks up one that's been torn in half- presumably of Martin Luther King- and says '**See this man? He says we mustn't fight. Says we can all live in peace. Says don't cause no trouble. [...] You see him? Well, they killed him. Yeah, shot him dead.**' The reader can see why Tufty is so frustrated- he has been trying to be peaceful, but he's still been attacked. He starts throwing more things around his shed, and then tells Leon to '**Stand up for yourself.**' He explains that he was brought up to be peaceful, but he seems to resent the message he was given.

At home, Leon can't sleep. He watches Blankety Blank with Sylvia, and then tells her that he say policemen fighting two black men. Sylvia just tells him to keep out of it. He then asks her to tell him more stories about the rabbit's adventures. Sylvia is a bit drunk, and tells him a rude story about a bear using the rabbit to '**wipe [...] his arse.**' Leon laughs, and '**Lean and Sylvia lie on the bed together, rolling from side to side.**' At the end of an emotive and highly tense chapter, we have a moment of comic relief, and are reminded that Leon is only a young child.

Questions
1. What do you think Leon wants the shed for?
2. How does the systemic racism seen in this chapter resonate with a modern reader?
3. What do you think Devlin means with the line, 'They're the same all over the world. Small minds, big feet.' Do you think his attitude towards the police in authority reveals anything about his past?
4. What could Tufty's gesture with the space symbolise?
5. Do you think Tufty is right- we need to fight and be violent to incite change?

Terminology
Idiolect- The style particular groups of people speak in

Essay Hint- Perspectives (AO3)
If you look at the mark scheme for AO3 (go to the AQA website), you'll see a clear difference between Level 2 and Level 3 for AO3- Level 2 requires you to show 'some awareness of implicit ideas/contextual factors', and Level 3 requires you to have 'some understanding of implicit ideas / **perspectives** / contextual factors shown by links between context/text/task. If you're considering how the ideas in this text resonate with a modern reader, you've made that vital jump between these levels.

Chapter 28

Summary

- A new social worker is coming to assess Leon. Sylvia wants to look nice for him as he's a man, and remember her ex-husband.
- When the social worker comes, he talks to Leon alone. It seems he doesn't really care about what Leon is saying.
- Leon gets angry when thinking about Jake. He runs into the bathroom, and makes a huge mess.
- Sylvia sends the social worker away, and Leon thinks he'll be asked to leave. He gathers his belongings.
- Sylvia makes him clean up his mess, and explains that they need to be together until Maureen comes back.

Analysis

Sylvia is hungover, and social workers are coming over early. She calls herself 'rough', and Leon makes a jokes about her pretending to be a dog. As the reader, we can see that their relationship is a lot more friendly and jovial than it was when Leon first moved in. The new social worker is a man, **'the boss of the boss'**, and Sylvia does her makeup specially. She comes out with lipstick on her teeth.

She explains that she used to be married- both she and Maureen (sisters) were married to a pair of brothers- **'She got the good one and I got the bast- git.'** Sylvia explains how he left her, both for another woman and in his head- **'Took leave of his senses, as they say. Cuckoo.'** This is derogatory slang for someone with mental health problems.

In another book, *Supporting Cast,* Kit de Waal develops the back stories of some of the characters in her novels. One of these is Sylvia, and you can read a bit more about her relationship with her husband.

The new social worker- Mike- arrives. It turns out he's the **'Independent Reviewing Officer for Leon.'** Leon calls him **'Earring'** as he has a single earring in the shape of a cross. As Sylvia goes to make him a coffee, he explains to Leon that he's there to listen to Leon, and make sure his **'needs are being met'**. He says, **'You're old enough to have your wishes and feelings taken into account and for you to tell us what those wishes and feelings are.'** For the reader, who has followed

Leon's wishes and needs through the story, it seems unfair that his wishes are only being taken into account now.

Kit de Waal explained that she chose the third person limited point of view for the story because, 'This is his story, so it had to be in his voice.' She said 'I have worked with lots of children in foster care, and so often their story is told by a social worker or their parent, or a foster carer or a guardian, anyone but the child. Even when social workers do their very best, it's not the same as hearing it from a child.' We see the unfairness of Mike's statement that it is only now that Leon is being given the chance to express his own wishes and needs.

During the discussion with Leon, it becomes evident that Mike is just asking this questions because it's part of his job- **'Earring speaks quickly, like he's running out of time. He asks all the questions the Zebra asks but faster, writing and talking or putting ticks in boxes. It goes on for ages, then he sits back and takes a breath.'** His dialogue is significantly longer than Leon's; Leon replies in one word answers- either a **'Yes'** or **'No.'** As Mike asks him a question about his mum, he remembers how his mum said **'I can't manage myself, let alone you.'** The poignancy of this memory compared to the clinical, brisk tone of Mike's questions demonstrates to the reader that Mike doesn't actually care about Leon or his answers.

Finally, Leon starts asking questions- he asks when he'll live with Maureen again, where his old toys are, and where Jake is. Mike explains his toys have been lost. Interestingly, Leon seems to group all social workers together- he says **'You said he would write to me.'** In the narrative, the social workers' names are only referred to by their nicknames- Leon seems to be dehumanising and deindividualizing them, as they don't treat him like an individual person.

Leon starts to cry when remembering Jake, saying **'He needs me. [...] Only I can look after him.'** Mike tries to justify the decision to separate them, but Leon gets angry. He looks at Mike's pen and thinks **'The end of the pen is like a little metal knife. It could be dangerous and it could kill someone.'** Metaphorically, the pen is dangerous- it is part of the social care system, and the forms for assigning children to different homes. This might remind the reader of the proverb, 'The pen is mightier than the sword.' However, Leon purely thinks of it physically-he imagines pushing the pen **'through the soft bit of his eye'** and writing on Earring's brain, **'I f***ing hate you. Black Power. From Leon.'** This is shocking to read with the profanity and violence from such a young child, but it demonstrates Leon's frustration and anger.

Leon goes on a tirade about Jake missing him, and when Earring starts to speak, **'Leon knows every word he's going to say [...] he will talk slowly using baby words because he thinks Leon is stupid, but whatever words social workers use they all mean the same thing.'** Leon gets angry, and runs to the bathroom. He puts a roll of toilet paper in the toilet, alongside a towel and Sylvia's dressing gown. He pulls the toilet seat of the toilet. As he looks in the mirror, he thinks he'll see the incredible hulk, but all he sees is himself: **'He is nearly ten and he is black and Jake is one and he is white. That's why Jake is adopted. That's what Maureen said and she's the only one who has never lied.'** This is the first time in the narrative that Leon has directly referenced his own skin colour- as he's gotten older, he's been taught that skin colour does matter in terms of how you're seen and treated. We can see how unfair the situation is through Leon's eyes, and how frustrating the white lies people have told him are.

Sylvia asks if he's okay, and Leon realises he's wet himself. Sylvia looks in, and leaves without talking to him. She has what sounds like an argument with Earring. Leon takes his jeans, trainers and pants off and gets into his tracksuit bottoms and school shoes. He thinks that **'Sylvia will tell him to leave. She always said she wouldn't stand for any nonsense.'** He starts to gather his rucksack to leave.

Earring leaves, and Sylvia comes into his room and asks **'What were you thinking?'** Leon looks into the garden, and has some memories of his mum and dad, including when his dad said he was rip the neighbour's dog's heart out. He cries, and picks up his bag to leave.

Sylvia, however, puts a no-nonsense voice on and says **'If you think muggins here is putting them pissy clothes in the washer and tidying up, you're mistaken.'** She makes him go to the bathroom and clean up, one step at a time.

In the kitchen, she asks if Leon's ever heard the phrase **'Don't s**t where you sit.'** Leon says no, and she explains it means **'Don't f**k up** a good thing.' She explains that they like each other, and Maureen loves both of them, so they will stay together until she's well. She says **'If that mincing p***k comes back here with any of his nonsense, I'll sort him out.'** Nowadays, we recognise 'mincing' as a homophobic comment, and she also swears. Although the reader appreciates that she wants to look out for Leon, a modern reader might disapprove of her homophobic language.

She says she's taking 50p a week off his pocket money for a new toilet seat, but also makes a comment to show she recognises he's stashed all the stolen money in his bag. She says after Leon has cleaned the floor, he will have to have a bath, although it **'serves you right'** that his legs are itchy. Then, she remembers how she wet the bed until she was 9, and Maureen stood up for her and stopped her getting in trouble for it. The chapter ends with Sylvia saying **'Hope she gets better.'**

Questions

1. Social workers seem to be presented in a bad light in this chapter. Are they seen as negative throughout the whole text?
2. To what extent do you think Sylvia's actions and parenting methods are good in this chapter?
3. Do you think the pen is mightier than the sword?
4. What does the revelation about Sylvia's past husband add to your understanding of her character?
5. Kit de Waal has said that out of all the characters, she thinks she is most like Sylvia. What does that suggest?

Terminology
Proverb- A short well known saying, generally offering advice.

Essay Hint- Analytical Verbs
When writing essays, using a variety of analytical verbs can help you to focus on AO2- methods and effects.
The writer: suggests / implies / conveys / highlights / explores / demonstrates / reiterates / emphasises / exaggerates / hints to...
The reader: thinks / feels / imagines / behaves / responds / infers / recognises / questions / reflects on / understands...

Chapter 29

Summary

- Sylvia is acting distant, and Leon is worried she's angry.
- He goes to the allotments, and Devlin teaches him about plants. When Leon says he wants to get stronger, he takes Leon into the shed to give him some dumbbells.
- When Devlin is distracted by Tufty shouting, Leon steals the gun.
- Tufty is angry as Devlin and the allotment committee are trying to evict Tufty because he's subletting the plot. Tufty says he's just looking after it whilst his father is away, and that this is racist discrimination. Devlin denies this.
- When Tufty sees Leon in the shed, he accuses Devlin of being a paedophile. He tells Leon to stay away from him.
- Leon takes the weights and gun to his shed, and pretends to shoot the door.

Analysis

Sylvia is acting distant, and Leon is worried she's upset about the incident. In his room, Leon recognises that he's getting bigger and stronger.

He cycles to the allotment, and Devlin shows him how the plants he helped plant are growing. He thinks his method, of planting straight in the soil, is better than Tufty's of planting seeds in trays. Devlin teaches him about some plants, and then asks how old Leon is. Leon replies that it's his birthday the next day, and Devlin comments that he's big for ten. When Leon says he wants to get stronger, he announces his intention of carrying bricks in his rucksack. Devlin says he has something more efficient than bricks, and leads him into his shed. He throws some things onto the ground- including the gun which shocks Leon- and then finds some dumbbells.

As Leon lifts them up and down, Devlin asks where he feels it, touching Leon's chest and back. This might make a reader feel uncomfortable. Devlin allows Leon to keep the weights, and he puts them in his rucksack.

Tufty sees this interaction, and shouts saying '**What the f*** is this?**' As Devlin is distracted, Leon finds the gun and puts it in his rucksack. As Leon leaves the shed, Tufty is waving paper around. It becomes evident that Devlin and the allotment committee are having Tufty evicted for subletting his plot, although Tufty thinks it's because of the police presence the other day. He says '**This isn't about no f***ing subletting. This is about racism, pure and simple.**' Devlin denies these claims, saying Tufty is being '**ridiculous.**' Tufty says that Devlin likes being in charge and pretending it's a jungle and he's a general.

Tufty then notices Leon, and pulls him towards him. He says '**I seen them pictures you got in there. Little boys on your shelf.**' He then tells Leon, '**Stay away from that man. He don't like black people unless they're under sixteen.**' He is accusing Devlin of being a paedophile. He then towers over Devlin, and explains that his father has gone home for six months and he will look after the allotment until his return; he's been coming to the allotment with him since he was five. Tufty then threatens Devlin, saying '**Next time, I don't play so nice. You get me?**' As he says this, he walks forward, so that Devlin retreats into his shed.

Leon goes to collect his bike, but recognises his bag is too busy. He goes back to his shed- which he calls his '**halfway house**'- and puts the weights on the table. The table breaks. He then takes the pistol from his rucksack, and points it at the door, pretending to shoot: '**Pouf.**'

This is a highly tense moment in the novel, both the climactic fight between Tufty and Devlin which has been building for a while, and the more subtle but ominous image of a 9-year old boy playing with a gun.

Questions

1. Why do you think de Waal chose this moment in the novel for a fight between Devlin and Tufty to reach a climax?
2. What do you think Devlin's intentions are with Leon?
3. What do you think is being foreshadowed by Leon taking the gun?

Chapter 30

Summary

- It's Leon's birthday, and he gets some Star Wars toys from Maureen and Sylvia. He also gets a card and a photo from Jake, and the photo has Jake's address on the back.
- At the allotments, Devlin has bought Leon a patch of land, a fork, and a trowel.
- Leon then goes with Tufty who shows him some Kung Fu moves, and says Leon should get him mum to take him to lessons.
- Before going home, Leon drops off some stolen supplies into the abandoned shed he calls the Halfway House.
- At home, Sylvia has arranged a tea party, but as Leon didn't want to invite any friends Sylvia has invited hers. They talks about the riots and Irish Hunger Strike, then about Leon's mum. Leon hates that they feel sorry for him.
- Later in bed, Leon asks if he can buy a map and a compass. Sylvia tells him an inappropriate story, and he goes to sleep.

Analysis

It's Leon's birthday. Sylvia has been too busy planning the street party for the royal wedding to talk to Leon, but he's still hoping to get some more Action Men for his birthday. He thinks of the Action Men he left behind at his home with Carol.

Sylvia greets him, saying, **'Ten years old and nearly looking me in the eye. Bloody hell! You've grown overnight, haven't you?'** She gives him a birthday kiss and presents from herself and Maureen. Sylvia has gotten him a Darth Vader toy- **'Darth Vader is evil and Leon wonders if he will have a bad dream if Darth Vader is in his bedroom.'** Leon's childish nature is juxtaposed with his mature appearance- he is a lot younger than he seems because of his height. Maureen has got him an AT-AT Walker which he's much more excited about.

Sylvia also gives him an envelope, and says **'You've been waiting on this and, between me and Maureen, we made sure you were going to have it on your birthday.'** Inside the envelope is a picture of Jake, looking older, and **'One arm is reaching out for Leon.'** He looks at the picture, but thinks '**Jake is smiling but Leon can see he's tired and he doesn't like having his picture taken.**' He knows the address will be on the other side of the picture, so he doesn't turn it over in front of Sylvia. There is also a letter, and Leon knows '**It isn't written by a baby, it's typed.**' Sylvia lets him pick whatever he wants from breakfast, and he opens all his cards.

Later, Leon goes into his room and looks at the address. He's angry as Jake has to sleep in a room by himself. He keeps moving the photograph into and out of his rucksack, then next to his bed. We sense his frustration that he's away from Jake.

At the allotment, Devlin is there watering his plants. He says he's got Leon a present, and takes him to a plot between his and Tufty's: '**It's overgrown and untidy; nobody looks after it.**' Devlin explains how it's about a quarter of a standard plot, and '**It now belongs to you. It's your small patch of the planet. It's arranged with the committee and I'm your sponsor.**' He also gives Leon a fork and a trowel and some scarlet emperor seeds, and explains that he's responsible for the land. He asks Leon what responsible means, and Leon says '**It's always there in your mind even when you can't see it because you're thinking about it all the time and you have to make sure it's safe and everything you do is about looking after that thing and making sure it's all right […] Because that's your job.**' This is a really touching quotation, which highlights Leon's caring nature.

Tufty arrives, and Devlin and he and stare at each other without talking until Leon tells Tufty about his present. Tufty says he needs more than just the trowel and fork, and takes him to his shed. Although Tufty and Devlin regularly clash, we sense that they both care deeply about Leon and want what's best for him, so here they put their differences aside. Leon thinks Tufty's plot is the third best in the allotment because of his raised beds. Tufty says he can't do hard work on his birthday, and gives him some pop.

Leon asks Tufty how he got his muscles, and Tufty says '**Just born this way,**' then, '**I used to do a bit of martial arts when I was young.**' He teaches Leon some Kung Fu moves, but explains that Kung Fu means 'hard work.' He says '**You do those moves every day and you get muscles. You get muscles and no one can f*** with you.**' Leon copies his moves, and thinks that '**Tufty moves like a cross between a soldier and a ballet dancer, graceful and dangerous.**' However, as Tufty does the moves he starts to get angry thinking about the police. He says '**When people f*** with you, you got a choice. You f*** back or you swallow down. [...] Swallow enough times and you start to choke. [...] Or you learn to accept. Let go. Breathe easy.**' We hear more about Tufty's philosophy here- he wants peace, both with others and himself, so he thinks he needs to learn to accept.

Tufty says that Leon needs martial arts lessons, and he should ask his mum and dad to take him. Leon doesn't want to talk about his 'parents', so says he has to go. He goes to '**the halfway house**' and puts things he's taken from Sylvia's house in there- tins of food, sugar, and a blanket. We've not been explicitly told what he wants these for, but we can guess that he's trying to make somewhere safe for himself, his mum, and Jake.

Back at Sylvia's, a tea has been set up. Sylvia has evidently been asking him to ask some other kids over, but Leon doesn't want to. She says '**You can bring some of your mates back here sometime if you like, you know. You should have friends, Leon.**' We sense she's concerned because she has never met any of the boys Leon keeps saying he plays with at the park- we know this is a lie, and he's going to the allotments.

As Leon doesn't have any friends around, Sylvia has some of hers over. Leon gets a lot more presents. The friends '**talk about riots in another city and the Irishmen that are dying on a hunger strike.**' These allusions seem to be to the Bristol or Brixton uprisings of 1981, and the 1981 Irish Hunger Strike. Interestingly, these events show people making the choice to '**f*** back**' (to use Tufty's words). They haven't '**swallow[ed] down**' or '**learn[t] to accept**', but are fighting back in two very different ways. By positioning these allusions near Tufty's philosophy, the reader can see some examples of different ways of dealing with unfairness in society.

The friends get into a small debate about the IRA, but Leon doesn't pay much attention to this as Sylvia starts saying '**Not one single word from his mother.**' She explains how hard she, Maureen, and Judy (the Zebra) had to fight to get the photo and card from Jake's family. She says '**Cheered him up it has, little soldier.**' She acknowledges Leon's strength, but in a patronising way. Leon can feel them looking at him, and thinks '**He knows what their faces look like and how they feel sorry for him and how much they hate his mum.**' He's angry, and wishes he was with his mum and Jake again. He remembers how Jake and Carol used to fall asleep, and '**Leon sits down next to Jake and looks at his perfect lips and perfect face.**' The slip into <u>present tense</u> suggests the power of Leon's memory.

That night, Leon asks Sylvia where Dovetail Road is. Sylvia says it's across town. Leon asks if he can buy a map and a compass, and Sylvia says '**You can buy what you like, love, it's your money.**' It seems ridiculous that Sylvia isn't more suspicious about why Leon wants these things, and the reader can probably work out he wants to find Jake.

He asks for a story, and Sylvia goes off on a rant about the bear who '**buggers off because bears are like that. They don't stay around when they're needed. [...] Bears are selfish and when they've had their fun, they barge their way back into the woods and disappear.**' This seems to be a metaphor for men, and we sense that Sylvia is upset and bitter about being alone. She then tells a story about a pig who saved a farmer's family, but the farmer still ate the pig's leg, and '**Leon decides he won't ask Sylvia for any more stories and he turns over.**' Again, we can see how Sylvia isn't being how we'd expect a typical carer to be.

Questions

1. In what ways is Leon's birthday an important stage in his development?
2. In what ways is Sylvia a good carer? In what ways is she a bad carer?
3. Do you think Tufty's philosophy in this chapter to '**f*** back [...] swallow down [...] or [...] learn to accept. Let go. Breathe easy**' is a good one? Why, or why not?
4. Do you think it's good that Leon has received the photograph and letter from Jake, or do you think he should be trying to forget about his brother? Why?

Terminology
<u>Present Tense-</u> Writing in the present, as if things are happening.

Chapter 31

Summary

- Sylvia makes Leon watch a film with a boy with special needs. He is embarrassed.
- Later, Leon goes to the allotments. His plot of land has been cleared up. He goes to Devlin's shed to look for more seeds.
- Devlin is sleeping, drunk. Leon has a flashback to the time he say his black granny before she died.
- Leon tries to touch Devlin's knife, but Devlin wakes up. He starts to whittle a model of Leon's head, and shows him his other models. He is drunkenly talking, and is remembering his son's death.
- Leon is scared, and when Devlin falls asleep he leaves. He plants his seeds, and goes to Tufty's shed to look for more.
- Tufty's shed is unlocked, and Castro is inside. He's been beaten up. He wants food or drink, and Leon says he knows where whiskey is.
- He goes back to Devlin's to pick up whiskey, and Devlin is still asleep. Leon also steals a pruning knife and Devlin's favourite carved head.
- He gives the whiskey to Castro but runs away, straight into Tufty.
- Tufty takes Leon backs to his shed and finds Castro. Castro explains how he was beaten up unfairly by police in the street, and he ran away.
- Leon promises not to say anything, and goes home.

Analysis

The next day, Leon goes to the cinema to watch *Raiders of the Lost Ark*. However, Sylvia makes him go with another boy: **'The boy is called Timmy and he is special.'** This is a <u>euphemism</u> for someone with special educational needs. Timmy is noisy during the film and Leon is embarrassed. As a reader, we recognise that Sylvia is concerned that Leon doesn't have friends and is trying to make him more sociable.

This interaction means that Leon is late to the allotments. When he gets there, he sees that his plot is neat- someone has weeded, made the paths neat, and made some wigwams. Leon thinks about the insects beneath the earth: **'Leon lies down on the earth and feels them marching and burrowing and making their nests and bumping into each other. Hello, spider. Hello, beetle.'** He wants the best plot on the allotment, but will need more seeds.

He knows Tufty isn't around, so goes to Devlin's shed. Devlin is drunk and sleeping on his chair, and Leon realises that he always wears the same clothes and smells, and '**sometimes Leon thinks that Mr Devlin might actually be a tramp.**'

Leon walks around and looks at his things, and sniffs a bottle of whiskey. It reminds him of '**his black granny that he only met once before she died.**' The granny had to have her feet amputated because of her diabetes, and Byron had never told her about Leon until she was dying. The granny told him to be a good son, and gave him five pounds. When she spoken to Byron, Byron said '**Sorry, Mommy**' and '**Leon's never heard that voice before. He's never heard his dad sound like a little boy.**'

Later, the granny died and Byron was drunk and hugging Leon repeating '**I got no one now.**' Leon can smell the same whiskey scent on Devlin.

Leon wants to touch Devlin's knife, but as his fingers reach it Devlin puts his hand on Leon's neck, and moves him away from the knife. He makes Leon sit on the floor, and says '**Thought we were friends.**' He picks up the start of a carving, and begins to whittle Leon's head. He gestures to a wall of carved things- animals, women, '**and then, at the very front, little heads of children. All boys.**' He recites the names of some of them, including someone we can infer was his son- Pedro Gabriel Devlin. Leon asks if they're his children, and Devlin giggles until he laughs so much he can't carve- '**What? All of them? Forty-seven children?**'

He explains that he used to work at a school and take some boys into his workshop to carve. He says, '**I was loved. They loved me.**' He takes Leon's hand and shows him how to carve the wood. Suddenly, there is a shift in atmosphere as Devlin '**grips his hand tighter**' and shouts, '**Keep the f***ing rules! Isn't that what I told him? Isn't it? Slow down, I said. Over and over, I said it. [...] Don't run!**' The reader doesn't yet know what Devlin is referencing, but can tell he's remembering something traumatic in his past.

He shows Leon four carved heads of the same child, but older each time. He says '**It's my fault, she said. My fault for shouting. He wasn't looking. My fault. Always my fault. Always will be my fault. For ever and ever. Amen.**' We get the impression that Devlin's son was ran over, and his wife blames him for shouting and distracting him, even though Devlin knows he always told the boy to slow down and not run. This revelation about Devlin's past is a key element to his character development- we can see why he has an odd relationship with children, and how his trauma and guilt might have led him to alcohol and bitterness. This also adds to the theme of guilt we have seen in the text, with Leon feeling guilty he's not looking after Jake.

Leon leaves as Devlin drinks more- '**He understands why Tufty doesn't like Devlin.**' He goes to his shed, and tries to tidy up a bit. He has bought more food- trifle mixes- and lists the things he'll need, including a bed and more food.

Back at his plot, he plants the Scarlet Emperor seeds and waters them. He wants to grow more, '**but doesn't want to spend any of his money on carrot seeds because he's going to need every penny.**' Together with his shed, the reader gets more hints that Leon is preparing to fetch his brother. He decides to go to Tufty's shed to collect some seeds, and sees that the lock is open.

However, when he goes inside the shed, Castro pulls him inside and '**shoves Leon against the wall so hard that the door slams and makes a noise.**' Castro looks beaten up- '**He has blood on his lips and one of his eyes is swollen and closed.**' He's clearly been staying in the shed- he's made a bed on the floor and has been drinking pop. Castro asks why Tufty hasn't been back to the shed, as he thought Tufty came to the allotment every day. Castro asks if Leon has food in his rucksack but he says no, thinking about '**his precious things and what he will do if Castro tries to take them.**' Castro says he needs a drink, and Leon says he can get him some whiskey.

Castro threatens him before he leaves, and Leon wonders '**Who is the worst, Castro or Mr Devlin?**' Mr Devlin is asleep, and Leon takes a bottle of whiskey. Leon is angry- '**he can feel the anger for Castro bubbling in his throat. It makes him want to smash the bottle against the wall. [...] It makes him want to take the big curved blade and march to Tufty's shed, kick the door off its hinges, and stab**

Castro and tell him to f*** off.' Leon also takes Devlin's carved baby head- **'the one Devlin talks to, the one he loves'** and a pruning knife.

Leon gives the whiskey to Castro, who gulps it quickly. Leon runs away from the shed, but **'something hits him in the face and he falls over.'** It's Tufty, and Leon **'likes the way Tufty looks worried and the way the lines have appeared on his forehead and his eyebrows are closed together.'** Tufty thinks Leon is running from Mr Devlin who has touched him, but Leon just says he's thirsty. Tufty says he'll get Leon some pop, but Leon **'tries to go slow.'**

When they get closer to the shed, Tufty sees the lock is broken and questions Leon about who is inside. Leon reveals it's Castro, and Tufty goes in. It turns out Castro is **'on the run'**. He reveals that he got a solicitor who was able to have Castro released **'on a technicality'**, and he was told he could sue the police for when a dog bit him **'last time'**. However, as Castro was turning to the solicitors, he reveals that **'Three police pull up in a beast wagon. Right there on the street they attack me.'** He says **'They don't usually beat you till they get to the station, but these people out of control.'** As the solicitor came out and saw this, Castro ran off.

Tufty tells Leon to go home, and Leon promises not to tell anybody.

Questions
1. Why do you think de Waal included the flashback to Leon's black granny?
2. Does this chapter make you sympathise with Devlin, or not?
3. Do you think Tufty would have minded if Leon had helped himself to some seeds from his shed?
4. Does this chapter make you sympathise with Castro, or not?
5. Why do you think Leon took Devlin's whittled head, despite knowing it was one of his most cherished possessions?

Chapter 32

Summary

- Leon remembers how upset Sylvia was when he came home late the previous week.
- Leon and Sylvia go food shopping. Leon overhears a conversation between Sylvia and a friend about how Maureen is still ill, and Sylvia wants her to stop fostering when she gets out of hospital.
- Leon steals some baby food, and thinks about all the other things he's going to need to steal.

Analysis

It's the bay Sylvia usually goes shopping, but as it's raining so much both Leon and Sylvia spend the day eating bread. The rain is described in detail: Leon **'looks at the silver raindrops weeping on the window.'** As he watches the raindrops racing, he imagines one is his and one is Jake's.

Leon and Sylvia can't decide what to watch. Sylvia is still angry with Leon about him coming home late the last weekend. She was frantic, asking questions without letting Leon answer, as **'there was some sort of aggro up on Nineveh Road.'** Again, we see that social unrest is the background of Leon's childhood. Leon had said he'd fallen off his bike and hurt his back, and Sylvia was initially sympathetic but since then has been angry.

Leon catches Sylvia watching him- she often does this, and **'Sometimes she looks soft and reminds him of his mum.'** We sense that Sylvia has become a lot more attached to Leon. She explains to Leon it's her birthday soon, and how she was very young- seventeen- when she got married. She asks Leon how old his mum is, but he doesn't know.

Leon asks if he can do the Kung Fu class on Carpenter Road, and Sylvia says she'll speak to his social worker about it. They then go shopping, taking the bus because of the rain. There is someone dressed as a bear outside, and **'Sylvia and Leon both think of the rabbit story and smile at each other. Sylvia even checks his bum as they walk past.'** Again, the pair seem to be getting closer. This is a huge <u>juxtaposition</u> to how Leon said he hated Sylvia at the start, and shows how getting to know someone can make you feel closer to them.

Leon asks to look at the toys, and then goes to find Sylvia. She's talking to a friend, and says '**Got used to the little bugger if I'm honest.**' She then talks about Maureen, who we learn had a stroke and an infection since she's been in hospital. Sylvia is determined Maureen will come and live with her when she's out, and that she won't keep fostering children, as '**[Social Services] are always giving her the worst kids with the most problems.**' As a reader, we're not sure if Sylvia intends to keep Leon or not.

Leon continues wandering, and goes into the baby food aisle. He steals some baby food, and '**makes a list of all the other things he will steal.**' He '**remembers the weight of Jake in his arms and the feel of his brother's arms around his neck, the fingers pulling his hair, the smell of him.**' Leon still clearly misses his brother, and is continuing his plan to 'rescue' him.

Questions

1. What do you think has made the biggest difference in Leon and Sylvia's relationship?
2. Do you think Sylvia intends to keep Leon when Maureen is out of hospital?
3. What do you think Leon's plan is, precisely?

Essay Hint- Language, Form, and Structure (AO2)

When writing essays, try to discuss language, form, and structure.

Language- imagery, vocabulary, dialogue, language devices, etc.
For example, in this chapter, we might look at the imagery of the raindrops racing down the window creating a sad and nostalgic atmosphere.

Form- HOW the story is told: third person limited perspective, bildungsroman genre, etc.
For example, because of the limited perspective, we don't know how much of the overheard dialogue Leon has actually understood.

Structure- The order in which we learn things, and how each chapter and event has been structured.
For example, the development of Sylvia and Leon's relationship, and how they have gotten closer since they first met.

Chapter 33

> **Summary**
>
> - At the allotment, Leon looks at the progress of his plants.
> - Tufty gives him some more seeds, and explains he has two daughters he doesn't see very much. As he's thinking about them, Leon plants the seeds.
> - Tufty reads a poem to Leon, called **'Ode to Castro.'** It's about black history and oppression, but ends powerfully saying black people are warriors because of their history.
> - At home, Leon thinks about the last time he saw his father. He was dropping off presents before his court date, and Carol didn't seem sad to see him go.

Analysis
Leon goes to the allotment, and looks at the progress of his seeds: **'They are so small and delicate, Leon wonders if they will survive. They shudder in his breath.'** He hints to Tufty he wants more seeds, and Tufty takes him into his shed. He makes up rhymes as he drops seeds in Leon's hand, and Leon makes a rhyme too.

Tufty explains he works in a bike shop for Mr Johnson. Leon asks if he has children, and Tufty says he has two girls who live far away with their mum; he doesn't get on with her. Leon tries explaining he has a brother, but Tufty is lost his memories: **'He's gone off to play with his little girls [...] He's smelling their hair and holding them.'** The power of memory is strong.

Leon plants the seeds and waters them. Then, Tufty reads him a poem he wrote- **'Ode to Castro.'** An <u>ode</u> is a lyric poem which praises something or someone, meant to be sung. The last stanza is particularly powerful:
> 'We have lost the way we used to live
> And the way that we behaved
> We are the consequence of history
> We are the warriors you made.'

The poem is about the oppression of black people, and is powerful and clever. It acknowledges the mistreatment of the past, and says that it is this that will make them stronger. In Chapter 20, Castro accused Tufty of only thinking about girls when he read his last poem, but here we can see that Tufty is using his words and language to protest what is happening- he is not just 'accepting', but fighting back peacefully.

When Leon gets home, he repeats the line '**We have dignity and worth.**' Tufty reminds him of his father- not the appearance or voices, but small mannerisms. Leon remembers the last time he saw his dad, on Christmas Eve. Carol was pregnant, and Byron was annoyed at her. He explained he'd heard that the baby's father had left Carol.

Byron's court date was coming up the next day, and he wanted to drop a few things off for Leon. His Christmas presents were tied in a bin bag, and Byron said he wasn't allowed to open them until the next day.

As he left, '**Leon wanted to be happy, but when he saw his dad walk away he wanted to run after him.**' Last time his father had been to court, his mum had been upset, '**but this time she didn't care.**'

Questions

1. Why do you think de Waal uses so much beautiful imagery when describing the plants?
2. How powerful do you think art can be as a form of protest?
3. Why do you think we're only hearing about Tufty's family now?
4. Which character seems to have the most powerful memories?

Terminology
Ode- A lyric poem praising someone or something

Chapter 34

Summary

- Maureen is coming home the next day, so Sylvia and Leon clean the house.
- Leon remembers all the bedrooms he's stayed in, and is hopeful he can return to his second bedroom with Maureen.
- Sylvia goes on a date, but is stood up. She is sad when she returns, but Leon comforts her saying that Maureen is coming home.

Analysis

Sylvia is on the phone to Maureen, and is told the news that she's being released from hospital the next day. Sylvia and Leon are excited- Sylvia is so excited that she doesn't paint her final two toenails and makes Leon help her clean the house ready for Maureen's arrival.

Syvlia scrubs the front-door step, remembering how her mum used to do it every Saturday morning. She talks to herself, saying '**The neighbours think you're mad. Mo thinks you're mad. You know it yourself. But that's who you are and there's no changing now.**' Here, we can see the theme of identity and self-acceptance. As she talks to herself, she gets Leon to fetch her a coffee, and Leon admits '**Sylvia has young eyes and sometimes he can see that she used to be pretty.**' In the novel, Leon has been obsessed with ideas about beauty- he didn't want to hold Maureen's hand in public in case people thought she was his mum, and he often links Carol to her beauty. Here, perhaps he is recognising that beauty isn't something permanent, or something that is just on the surface. He seems to be maturing.

Sylvia gets dressed up, and Leon remembers all of his bedrooms. He thinks now that Maureen is coming home he can live at hers again. It is nice for the reader that he counts Sylvia's house as one of his bedrooms (he did not count the previous foster families he stayed with or Tina's), but also the reader reognises that this may be a naïve dream and not possible.

Sylvia says that she's going out, and '**Crazy Rose**' looks after him but falls asleep, after continuously calling him Pete. When Sylvia returns home, Leon is still watching TV. She sends Crazy Rose home, then tells Leon (who she jokingly calls Pete) **'Bastard didn't turn up'**. She has evidently been stood up for a date.

She drunkenly says **'We're going to move to the seaside, that's what we're going to do. Me and Mo.'** Although this could just be Sylvia's drunken rambling, in which she imagines moving away from inconsistent men with her sister, it makes the reader (and assumably Leon) concerned because her dream does not involve him. Leon makes her another coffee, but Sylvia starts crying, and **'he holds her hand because that's what she did when he started crying when he was sick.'** We can see how Leon, as a child, learns behaviour- he imitates her method of comfort as he thinks that's what she would like. She apologies, but he reassures her saying **'Maureen is coming tomorrow.'** We can see how much Leon depends on Maureen, and thinks she will make everything right.

Questions

1. What ideas about hopes and dreams does this chapter communicate?
2. What seems to be Sylvia's attitude towards men?
3. In what ways has Leon matured as a character in this chapter?

Essay Hint- Tone, Atmosphere and Mood (AO2)

Having a variety of words to discuss tone, atmosphere and mood, and subsequent shifts, is key. For example, in this chapter it starts with an **optimistic and excitable** atmosphere, before the tone to describe Sylvia's actions becomes more **manic and erratic.** At the end, the atmosphere is more **despondent and sad,** as Sylvia cries about her evening. It ends with a **poignant optimism,** as Leon hopes that Maureen's return will make everything better.

More words to describe atmosphere, tone, and mood: critical, cynical, foreboding, ominous, tense, bitter, detached, hopeful, subversive, relaxed, joyous, etc.

Chapter 35

Summary

- In the morning, Leon checks his rucksack but things he may not even have to go through with his plan if Maureen is back and he's living with her.
- However, Leon feels betrayed by Sylvia when she explains that she's hoping Maureen will live at Sylvia's house for good.
- When Maureen arrives, it's initially good- Leon and her hug, and Leon thinks that everything will be back to how it was before. However, she and Sylvia discuss the possibility of moving into a beach cottage together. Leon feels betrayed, but pretends he's okay. He feels his rucksack again, and decides he can manage it on his bike.
- As Leon listens to the sisters discussing future plans, a news report comes on TV. There are riots and looting following the death of a man in custody.

Analysis

As Sylvia has been drinking, Leon knows she will be sleeping late. Leon **'looks through every single thing he's collected and all the things he has in his rucksack.'** This includes money, food, seeds, tools, maps, soap, the photograph of Jake, and some more concerning things like **'the gun'** and **'a knife'** casually placed alongside the day-to-day items. This is shocking to a reader, as we know that Leon is not mature enough to have weapons about his person. He is checking because he thinks he's going straight to Maureen's house and will need the things there. We are even more curious about his plan when it says, **'Leon might have to wait to do his plan now that Maureen's back. He might not have to do it at all.'**

However, when Sylvia is awake, she apologises for what she was saying the night before (even though she can't quite remember what she said). She says **'Mo will be here sometime today. I'm hoping she'll move in for a few days. Or even for good.'** Leon is shocked, and spills some hot water over himself as he thought he would be moving back in with Maureen, like before. He decides she can make her own coffee for herself as she's **'talking rubbish.'** Like his stealing, this seems to be another way Leon finds to punish the adults who betray him.

Maureen finally arrives, and gives Leon a huge hug, saying '**I've needed a good hug, I have. That's better than all the tablets in the world.**' They eat cake, although Sylvia makes Maureen promise it will be her last cake as she eats too much sugar. When Sylvia is calling Leon 'Pete', she has to explain to Maureen it's a joke that Crazy Rose started. Maureen imitates Crazy Rose, and everyone laughs.

Leon asks if he can go out on his bike, and Maureen seems a lot more sceptical about it than Sylvia. She says she'll want to see it the next day. As Leon goes to wash before leaving, he overhears Maureen and Sylvia's conversation- Sylvia explains how he's a '**good kid, all in all**'. They discuss his size and appearance, and '**Leon smiles and feels the muscles at the top of his arms.**' Despite the uncertainties about Leon's future living arrangements, the atmosphere seems happy and optimistic.

However, they start discussing the future, and Sylvia declares to Maureen '**You're moving in with me.**' She says they can split the bills, and look after each other now that they're older. Sylvia discusses her plan to move by the sea, and Maureen says she can think of many reasons not to go. Sylvia says '**Just give the idea a chance for a few minutes, Mo. Stop thinking of why not all the time.**' Maureen is quiet for a while, and then '**her voice is different, it's all soft like when she used to tell Jake a bedtime story.**' She goes off into a dream about living by the sea, and all the things they could see and sense. She asks, in a *wistful (contemplative, thoughtful)* tone, '**What is it about the sea? What is it when you look out at the sea and feel calm?**' They talk about the dog that they can get and the '**Sound of the waves at bedtime**,' and Sylvia concludes it saying '**Just you and me, Mo.**'

Leon flushes the toilet, spits, and flushes again. He feels angry and betrayed. He goes into his room, feeling sick- '**He feels all his blood turning to clay, feels Sylvia's plans settle like an anchor on his chest.**' This <u>figurative language</u> shows the reader the extent of betrayal Leon feels, and he imagines he can feel his mum's hands on his hands, '**her stained fingers, brown as rotten fruit.**' The use of rotten imagery suggests that he feels like all the adults in his life are corrupt and liars, and '**deep in his brain, he can hear something screaming and wailing, the new realisation that Maureen is just like everyone else.**'

He feels his rucksack, and thinks he can carry it to his shed. He goes into the adults, and Maureen says she'll walk to the park with Leon, but Leon says he will stay with her: **'He smiles. Just like Maureen has a soft voice and Sylvia has three or four different voices, Leon can have a pretend voice as well.'** Now he feels betrayed by the one adult he's thought he can trust, he feels like he can lie effectively now. Whereas his other lies are recognised, this one isn't.

However, **'Then, the whispering begins.'** Sylvia and Maureen go into the kitchen, and they're discussing telling Leon something. Maureen says she wants to wait until the **'permanent'** thing that's happening is **'official'**, and all Leon can think is that they **'both want to get a dog instead of him.'** As a reader, perhaps being familiar with the terminology of adoption, we might think that Leon has misunderstood and that he is going to be adopted. However, Leon can only think about the negative consequences of this conversation.

Suddenly, both sisters run into the living room to listen to a news flash on the TV. It is revealed that there are **'clashes between police and gangs of youths following the death in custody of a local man from the union road area. What began as a peaceful demonstration outside Springfield Road Police Station has escalated into running battles between police and rioters.'** Police forces are being sent from other areas to support the police.

Questions

1. What plan do you think Leon makes in this chapter? What evidence is there for it?
2. What plans do you think Maureen and Sylvia are discussing in the kitchen at the end of the chapter?
3. The peaceful protest has turned to rioting. How do you think this happened?
4. We're only 7 chapters from end of the novel. What do you think will happen?
5. Why do you think Leon thought of his mum as he considered Maureen's betrayal?

Chapter 36

> **Summary**
>
> - There is a fire somewhere, and Leon can smell the smoke. He climbs out of his bedroom window, and cycles to the allotment. His face is swollen from the smoke and his crying.
> - He has a plan to cycle to Jake and take him back to his shed, and collect his mum from Bristol to live together. He thinks everything he's stolen in his rucksack will help.
> - At the allotments, Leon hears shouting. It transpires through Tufty and Devlin's argument that Castro has been beaten to death by police which has instigated a riot. Devlin wants Tufty to help him fix the allotment gate which has been ripped off by the rioters.
> - In their argument, Tufty accuses Devlin of being a paedophile. Devlin gets really worked up and starts throwing things around his shed. He's looking for his 'baby', Gabriel. Tufty is concerned, and tries to calm Devlin down.
> - Leon goes to his shed, but is scared. He imagines which might be in the dark. He runs out, but the door slamming is noisy. The argument stops.
> - Leon goes back in, and hears people creeping up. The shed door opens.

Analysis
The chapter begins with a series of short sentences- **'It smells like bonfire night. There's a feeling in the air like when something exciting is going to happen.'** De Waal's use of pathetic fallacy creates a shift in tone- after the perceived betrayal and despondency of the previous chapter, we are now told that **'Leon has done a brave thing'**- he's crept out of his window with his rucksack. Leon doesn't recognise the danger of sneaking out when there are riots, but the reader recognises from the smell of fire that there has probably been arson and looting happening. They worry for Leon.

Leon thinks that Maureen and Sylvia won't notice his disappearance as they're so engrossed in the TV. As he cycles, **'His face feels funny and his lips feel swollen from crying.'** He thinks about how sad Maureen and Sylvia will be when they find out he's gone, but **'it will be too late.'**

As he cycles, his throat and eyes get worse from the smoke. There are sirens and people standing around on corners, and some shout for him to stop. He continues.

He then worries that Jake won't remember him. He's grateful for the nail file he stole from Crazy Rose, as he thinks he'll be able to file away locks to get Jake out. He plans to drop off the heavy things at his 'halfway house' and then pick up Jake- if Jake can't walk and he can't steal a buggy, he plans on putting him in his rucksack. All of these plans- the film-esque filing through locks and the idea he can carry a baby in his rucksack- emphasise Leon's naivety. The reader feels concern about his plans, particularly with the background of rioting and arson Kit de Waal has established.

He then plans to find Carol. He thinks about how **'Every social worker he's ever had has told him that his mum loves her children but she just can't manage. Well that is going to change.'** He thinks about how much he has learnt since he last lived with her, including **'how much things cost and how to take them cleverly when you haven't got enough money.'** He then thinks of the mistakes he made last time he was with Carol, like asking for help. He thinks they can manage together for weeks if they all stay together.

At the allotment, the gate is unexpectedly open and off its hinges. He hears shouting, and is initially *reticent (reluctant)* about going in, but then realises it's Tufty and Devlin. They're having an argument about the protest, and Tufty says **'It's a protest. Except we don't bomb people in their beds like you Irish people.'** Devlin says, **'Oh, every Irishman is a terrorist, is that what you're saying?'** Ironically, as Tufty is wanting to fight back about the prejudice and hatred the black community has received, he's attacking Devlin with negative stereotypes.

Tufty accuses Devlin of sitting in his shed drinking, ignoring what is going on in the world. He then says **'You think it's funny that the police kill black people?'** He reveals that Castro was killed in custody- **'They took him to the police station for some bulls**t reason and kicked him to death.'** The reader is shocked- the last we heard of Castro was in Chapter 33 when Tufty read his 'Ode to Castro' poem, of fighting and dignity and hope.

Devlin has been drinking, but says **'I'm sorry about your friend [...] but that doesn't mean they should be running through here like this.'** Leon looks around, and sees that the allotments have been trampled. Beds and plots have been destroyed. Tufty asks Devlin, **'You ever been angry? [...] I mean down in your belly. You ever been angry in your balls?'** He's communicating the frustration and anger of black people, who have been systemically oppressed and mistreated. When Devlin replies that he has been angry, Tufty asks **'Anybody make you into a slave? Put you in chains?'**

Devlin is frustrated and asks Tufty to help him fix the gate. He calls Tufty a **'child'**, and says **'don't make excuses for them [...]. They're savages.'** Tufty takes offence to this, and asks **'You calling black people savages?'** They fight, and Devlin cries out as he falls onto the ground. Tufty says **'I'd rather be a savage than a pervert. You think I ain't seen your pictures and your dolls?'** They fight again. Leon wants the torch they dropped so that he won't be as scared.

Tufty talks about Devlin's gifts to Leon, and insinuates he wants **'a piece of the real thing'** rather than just photos. Devlin continues shouting at Tufty, as Leon army crawls trying to find the torch. Devlin says **'I'll show you'**, and goes into his shed. Tufty stands at the entrance shining his torch, and Leon **'can see Mr Devlin through the window acting like he's gone mad. [...] He is staggering and bawling'**, and throwing his belongings off the shelves.

Leon soon realises he's looking for the carved head of **'Gabriel'** that is in his rucksack. Devlin shouts **'My baby, my son, where are you?'** Tufty is clearly concerned, and tells Devlin to **'calm down'** before going into the shed.

Leon runs with his rucksack to his shed. He is clearly panicked, as the physical state of him is described- **'His scalp is itching, his back is itching, [...] his chest is thumping so hard it might break open, his heart will jump and them Maureen will look for him and be sorry [...] and he won't care because he'll be dead.'** The length of the sentence emphasises Leon's panic and despair.

He can still hear the men shouting over the sirens, but he hears a scratch at his feet and imagines that **'Creatures and spiders might live in here, rats, [...] people, ghosts.'** He imagines that things are in the shed that **'could grab him and attack him like his nightmares. Kill him. Eat him. Tear him apart.'** He runs out from the shed, and the door slams. The men go quiet.

Leon remembers the cries of his father at his black granny's funeral, and wishes it were his father in the shed. However, he recognises that it was his father's attitude towards Carol that was partially responsible for the situation he's now in.

Leon can hear the wails of sirens, but also **'something coming close, soft and careful.'** He wants to go back in the shed, but thinks **'What if Castro has climbed out of his grave and it's him that's roaming around the allotments?'** We can see the power of a child's imagination here. He then imagines the sound is the police, coming for him. He climbs into the shed, and **'In the gloom, he can just see his rucksack. He reaches his hand out. The door flies open.'** The chapter ends on a cliff-hanger.

The rucksack seems to be a symbol for Leon's hope for the future- he reaches out to it for reassurance, but can't quite reach it.

Questions
1. Why does Leon seem to feel satisfaction at the idea of Maureen and Sylvia feeling upset about his disappearance?
2. Pick three moments of panic in this chapter. How does de Waal create panic? Consider words and phrases, sentence forms, and language features and techniques.
3. What do you think is the significance of the flashback to his black granny's funeral?
4. Why do you think Leon imagines Castro coming out of the ground to haunt him?

Terminology
Cliff-hanger- Ending a chapter or section on a moment of high tension

Chapter 37

Summary

- The shed opens, and Tufty and Devlin are there.
- Devlin sees the carved head which has fallen out of Leon's rucksack. Tufty tells Leon to apologise.
- Leon refuses, and goes into an outburst about how everyone can steal from him, and it's not fair.
- Leon takes the pruning knife out of his rucksack, and threatens Tufty and Devlin. They stand aside and let him leave the shed.
- As Leon hides, the men look for him. They start to fight about race and the riots, but Tufty refuses to engage.
- Leon makes a run for it, and Tufty and Devlin shout after him.

Analysis

The shed door opens, and it's Tufty and Devlin. Tufty pulls Leon up, but the carved head Leon stole from Devlin has fallen out of the rucksack. Devlin starts shouting at Leon, saying '**You stole him. He's all I have.**' Tufty tells him off for stealing as well, and Devlin cradles the head and asks '**How would you like it if someone took something from you? […] Something precious.**' Tufty tells Leon to apologise to Devlin.

However, when Leon looks up '**Their faces look strange in the torchlight. They are devils.**' He imagines their faces morphing into everyone he knows- '**Every face he has ever seen starts crowding into the shed. He can hear them breathing, thinking about what they will do to him in the long term and the short term […] and whispering about how to get rid of him so they can get a dog.**' In this extract, we recognise how little control Leon has over his own life- all the way through the text, adults have controlled what he has done and how he will live, and the reader recognises how awful this has been for Leon, and how terrible it must be for the many children in the social care system who feel like they have no control.

Leon pulls away from Tufty, and starts to put his rucksack on. Tufty says to say sorry and he'll take Leon home. Leon, however, says he's not sorry. Devlin gets upset and starts shouting again: '**My son is dead. Dead, do you hear me?**' Tufty recognises that Leon doesn't look well, and tells Devlin to leave it. Devlin though pulls Leon's arm and demands an apology. Tufty asks Leon why he's out so late and why he doesn't have a top on. However, **'Leon feels his teeth sharpening themselves against each other. He can hear the sawing in his temples, the grinding in his ears.'** He tells Tufty and Devlin, **'I don't care.'** Leon **'screws his fingers into tight fists and shoves his hand in the air like black power'**, saying **'No one cares about me. No one cares about my brother. I've got a baby as well. He's my baby. […] I can't see him. I keep asking and asking but you only care about yourself. Everyone steals things from me.'** This outburst is clearly an outpouring of repressed and frustrating from everyone who has not told him the truth or treated him well in the past.

Devlin and Tufty are silent, watching him. Leon says **'Anyway, I don't care because I can look after myself. And I can look after my brother.'** He becomes more confident in himself- **'He is tall. He's strong and powerful.'** He says the head doesn't look like Jake's head, and he has everything he needs to survive. However, when Devlin tries to speak, Leon pulls the pruning knife out of his rucksack and slashes it towards them. Devlin and Tufty tense up, and Leon enjoys the feeling of power he has.

The men are clearly scared, and back away. Devlin tries negotiating calmly, saying **'Leave him. The boy is right. He is in charge. He has the weapon.'** Devlin asks what his plan is, and Leon says he's going to Dovedale Road to get his brother, and then Bristol to the hallway house to collect his mother. Devlin says it's a long way and Leon will need someone with him, but Leon says he's going to leave straight away. Devlin suggests putting his clothes on first, or having something to eat or drink. Leon refuses, and thinks about what he's learnt from *Dukes of Hazzard*- **'If you want to get away, you have to keep your weapon on the enemy at all times.'** However, Tufty and Devlin don't move as Leon backs away from the shed.

As soon as Leon is out, the men start to follow him, but Leon **'crouches low like a soldier, stopping every so often. Crouch, stop. Crouch, stop.'** The lines between fantasy and reality seem to be getting blurred, as we remember how much of a child Leon really is. He thinks they're angry at him, but the reader knows they're more likely to be concerned.

As Tufty and Leon are shouting after him, it transpires that neither of them know Leon's name. They get into a brief argument about calling black children 'boy', but they spread out and hunt for him. He hides, but needs to get his bike before he leaves. Tufty recognises **'When you're desperate, you do desperate things.'** Conversation turns briefly back to the riots, and Devlin criticises it saying **'You have no plan, no structure, no chain of command...'** Leon hopes they argue again so they're distracted and he can leave.

However, Tufty starts to laugh, and says **'I ain't fighting you, man. [...] I'm not a fighter. I don't hate people. I'm not fighting no more.'** We sense that Tufty has found some sort of peace with his personal ideology on fighting. Tufty says Leon will come out for him, and starts to hunt again.

Leon makes a dash for his bike, but Tufty grabs it. Leon leaves by foot instead, Tufty and Devlin shouting after him.

Questions
1. Does it surprise you that neither Tufty or Devlin know Leon's name? What significance does this have when you consider the title of the book?
2. Do you think Leon's justification for not caring about stealing Devlin's carved head is right?
3. In what ways does Leon seem mature in this chapter? In what ways does he seem naïve?
4. What do you think has made Tufty come to the realisation that he's not a fighter?
5. This climax of the book is very late- do you think it's too late?

Chapter 38

> **Summary**
>
> - Leon runs through the streets, panicked and scared. He wants to get to Jake.
> - The streets are mostly abandoned, but show signs of a recent riot. A few men in turbans try to get Leon to leave the streets. He decides to go back for his bike.
> - Going down an alleyway, he emerges in the middle of a crowd of police and black men. Feeling panicked and trapped, he grabs the gun out of his rucksack. He points it at both groups of men.
> - As people start coming closer, he hears Tufty's voice.

Analysis

Leon is running, confused about his emotions. There are lots of other men and boys running, and '**He wants to fight them all. He wants them to stop and help him.**' Here, towards the climax of the book, we can see that the subplot of the riots is meeting the main plot of Leon's journey to find his brother.

Leon realises he smells of smoke, and he thinks of how Sylvia would tell him to have a bath, then make him sit down with crisps and a drink in front of the TV, and how she wouldn't be worried about where the smoke came through and Maureen would be.

He looks for his map, but pop has smashed in his rucksack and the map is wet. Something explodes, and he crouches next to a shop with smashed windows. De Waal describes how '**An angry ghost of black smoke rolls up the street. If Leon stays where he is, it will cover him up, eat him.**' We empathise with his panic and distress. He wonders if, when he finds Jake, the family will want another boy to look after. He promises to himself that if they take him in, he won't do any of the bad things like eavesdropping or stealing again.

Around a corner, Leon sees a car on fire, and hissing. He runs another way but the street is deserted. Down another street, the streetlights are off but there are men in turbans, who shout for him to come to them and out of the street. Leon runs away- he wants to fetch his bike from the allotments.

He runs down an alley, seeing a bright light at the end. He runs towards it, and emerges in the middle of a wide road **'and the noise turns itself on light a tap.'** There is a bike in the middle of the road, but as he approaches it he's in the middle of a group of black men and policemen. A bomb flies over his head, and he sees **'crowds and crowds of black men at the end of the street, surging forward and back like one wild lion about to pounce.'** The metaphor shows a display of unity, but a primal, angry, and aggressive unity against oppression. On the other side **'there's a wide wall of shields and truncheons, hundreds of policemen lined up across the street.'**

The police speak through a loudspeaker, telling the men to disperse. The men shout back, calling the police '**Racists! Killers!'** and other things. Leon is in the middle, crying. Bricks land near him, and he shouts for '**Dovedale Road.'** No one hears him- **'His words are drowned. The voices of the black men rise and snarl together like a monster's roar that carries right over Leon's head.'** He feels like no one is listening to him and no one knows where he is: **'No one is listening. No one ever listens.'**

Leon opens his rucksack, and takes out Devlin's gun: **'The policemen have truncheons and shields. The angry men have bricks and shouting. Leon has a gun.'** He points it at the police and then the black men in turn. Everything goes quiet, and then both groups shout for him to put the weapon down. As readers, we think this is a real gun, until the line **'Mr Devlin has done a good job with this gun'**, where they might suspect it's another one of his carvings.

As people approach, the dialogue gets shorter and tension builds. However, **'Then Leon hears one voice, clear and sweet above all the others.'** The call of **'Yo, star!'** shows the reader it's Tufty.

Questions
1. What foreshadowing has de Waal used to suggest the story might end this way?
2. What is the effect of the subplot and main plot joining?

Terminology
Subplot- A secondary story that happens alongside the main plot.

Chapter 39

Summary

- Leon waves at Tufty, and everyone drops down as he still has the gun in his hand.
- Devlin explains the gun is wooden, and tries to take it off Leon. Someone shouts that he's a 'pig', and he's injured by flying bottles.
- Tufty helps him up, and he and Leon try to get him back to the alley. However, Tufty is attacked by a policeman who beats him on his back with the truncheon.
- The policeman is about to hit Leon, but he stands up and recites 'Ode to Castro.' He then offers the policeman his hat, and asks for help. The policeman is rude, but lets them go.
- They stumble through the alley, and after going down a few streets, Leon recognises College Road, and tells the men he lives there.

Analysis

Leon is relieved to see Tufty, and waves at him- **'Leon raises the gun to wave and everyone drops to the floor.'** This is a moment of dark humour, as Leon's innocent waving contrasts with the consequences of waving around a weapon.

Then, Devlin runs out and shouts to the crowd that the gun is wooden. He goes towards Leon, asking for the gun. Leon backs away. As he grabs for Leon, bottles fly towards them and one hits Devlin in the face. The people shout **'Pig'**, a derogatory term for a police officer. More and more missiles fly towards them. Devlin shouts for Leon to run, and then something else hits him and he collapses.

The police and rioters start running towards each other, with Leon, Tufty and Devlin in the middle. Tufty tries to pull Devlin up, but he **'is swaying and won't move.'** Tufty asks Leon to help, **'but they can't get Mr Devlin up and there are people screaming, rushing past them from both sides.'** Finally, Leon throws down the gun and helps Mr Devlin up. They both encourage him to walk back to the alley, with a soundscape of the **'battle'** behind them. However, **'suddenly Tufty goes down.'** There is a policeman behind with a truncheon, and he hits Tufty over and over again on his back, shouting racist slurs. His helmet flies off with the force of his attack. Leon shouts for the policeman to **'Leave him'**, and the policeman raises his truncheon to hit Leon- **'He's panting, his mouth open in a horrible shape.'**

However, **'Leon holds his arms open. "We are not a warrior", he says. "We have dignity and worth."'** The policeman stops, stunned, as Leon recites Tufty's poem. This is evidently not what he was expecting. Leon explains to the policeman how they've been growing things in the allotment. De Waal describes the sounds of the battle around them, and the panic and chaos, **'But right now, in this place, there is no one else.'** Leon recognises that the policeman is scared. He thinks **'The policeman wants to say "Can you help me?" so Leon says it for him.** He fetches the man's hat for him, and offers it up, asking **'Can you help me?'** This is a touching moment- Leon fights back with innocence, and a reminder that police are there to protect people.

The policeman grabs the helmet, and tells Leon to **'F*** off.'** However, the danger is alleviated slightly. Leon helps Tufty up, pulling at him until he stands. They manage to pull Devlin up together, and stumble through the alley. They get to the next road, and Tufty says they have to get off the street. They go down the next road, and Leon recognises it- **'I live there [...] There [...] Right there.'** Leon knows that he can go to Sylvia's when he is in trouble.

Questions
1. Why do you think the policeman behaves in this way?
2. What do you think it was about Leon's actions that caused the policeman to stop?
3. Do you think that this is a satisfactory end to the riot?
4. How do people act differently in crowds to individually?

Terminology
<u>Dark humour-</u> A style of comedy that makes light of serious subject matter

Chapter 40

Summary

- Sylvia answers the door to Leon, and shouts to Maureen that he's back.
- Sylvia takes Devlin inside to dress his wounds, and Maureen makes Tufty come in. She speaks to Tufty but not Leon.
- Leon goes for a wee, and when he comes back Maureen finally speaks to him, asking if he's hungry. When Leon says yes she shouts, explaining how worried she and Sylvia have been.
- She calms down and gets some sandwiches. Leon eats then is told to wash and sleep in Maureen's room so he can't leave again.
- When Leon wakes, he remembers hearing the adults talking. He's hungry, so he leaves the room.

Analysis

Leon knocks on the door, and Sylvia answers in a panic, shouting '**It's him! Mo! It's him! Mo!**' The repetition and exclamatory sentences emphasise how much both sisters have been worried about Leon's disappearance. Sylvia pulls Devlin in.

When Maureen appears, '**Her face is red and her lips are moving but there are no words.**' Leon positions himself near Tufty, thinking that he can potentially ask to stay with him for one night before finding Jake if Maureen is too angry. Tufty touches the back of his head and sees blood, before telling Maureen to keep a closer eye on Leon. Maureen asks who he is, and Leon replies '**He's Tufty Burrows. He's a gardener.**' Tufty starts to walk away, but Maureen tells him to come in so that she can help and figure out what has been happening.

Maureen keeps up a monologue as she talks to Tufty and wipes his head- '**all the time talking and not looking at Leon.**' Sylvia is busy looking after Devlin. When she mentions getting the police involved, Devlin says no- '**I don't want the police. I saw what they did to him.**' He thanks Tufty for saving him.

Leon takes off his rucksack, and goes to the toilet. He looks at himself in the mirror- he is dirty and dishevelled, and has blood on his chest. He considers going back out, but it's dark and **'He might get hit by a rock or a policeman.'** This short sentence, together with Devlin's phrase from before, demonstrates how quickly faith can be lost in the institution.

When he goes back in, Maureen is ushering Tufty to a sofa in the living room and telling him to sit down, as it's not safe enough to go back out. She finally talks to Leon, and in a very typically Maureen way asks **'Have you had a wee? You'll need a sandwich before bed. Bet you're starving aren't you?'** Leon notices that **'her voice sounds very shaky and thin.'** Leon says yes, but Maureen stamps around and says **'What the bloody hell are you playing at, Leon?'** She explains how worried she and Sylvia have been, and how she's been calling the police who have been too busy to help. She didn't want to call social services as she thinks they would take him away saying she can't look after him properly.

Sylvia tells her to calm down, and Maureen goes into the kitchen. She comes out with sandwiches and tea for Tufty and says **'You're back. That's enough for now.'** Tufty makes him say sorry to Maureen, and Leon reluctantly does. Maureen says Leon has to wash, and then sleep on the floor in Maureen's room- the window is painted shut and she's going to put the dressing table in front of the door so Leon can't run away again.

In the morning, Leon wakes up to Sylvia laughing and the sun through the curtains. He can remember going to bed and hearing the adults laugh- or argue- but he fell asleep and didn't dream. He leaves the room, hungry.

This whole chapter has domestic conflict, contrasting with the **'civil war'** as Maureen described the physical and political conflict of the previous chapter.

Questions

1. Why do you think it took Maureen so long to speak to Leon?
2. Some people describe this chapter as a bit of an anti-climax. What do you think?

Chapter 41

Summary

- Maureen takes Leon to Bristol to see Carol.
- Carol explains that she cannot look after Leon anymore, and says he needs to stay with Maureen and not run away. As she turns to walk away, Leon asks if she still loves Jake. She replies that she loves him.
- On the train on the way home, Maureen gives an anecdote about how she once broke her arm and had a bad summer- sometimes, we go through bad periods in life, and this is one of Leon's bad times.
- She then explains that she has arranged for Leon to live with her permanently- he just needs to promise to tell her when something is wrong and never run away. Leon agrees.

Analysis

There is evidently a shift in time as we reach the **penultimate** *(one before last)* paragraph, as it doesn't address any of the consequences of the night before, but instead begins '**Something's different about Maureen.**' We learn she's been living with Sylvia who has been looking after her and making her eat healthy. In this chapter, she gets herself and Leon dressed up in their best clothes, and has been very quiet.

They have been on a train, and have had chocolate from the cart and played some cards. They are going to Bristol. Once off the train, they get a taxi and walk, seeing '**a massive battleship**', which we can assume is the SS Great Britain. Leon asks to look at it, but Maureen says '**Later**' and Leon thinks '**That's her favourite word of the day.**' They sit and have some sandwiches, and Leon infers they will be there a while because of the amount of food she's bought.

Maureen tells Leon to look at the river, and Leon imagines living on the battleship: '**Leon sees himself, sweaty, covered in black oil in the belly of the boat.**' He imagines destroying German U-boats and '**all the sailors cheer and cheer and the other men slap Leon on the back because they are safe.**' His daydreams are still about saving others and being a hero.

When he wakes from his daydream, Maureen says there's someone to see him- it's his mum. Leon runs over, and Carol comments on his height. Initially, it seems okay, but **'She takes his hand and squeezes it but as soon as they sit down, she puts both hands flat on the bench next to her. She starts to stroke the wood with her yellow fingers, picking out splinters and smoothing them down again. Her arms are skinnier than before.'** She is clearly still unwell, and is anxious about seeing Leon.

Leon asks if she's okay, and she says '**Anyway, it's me that should be asking how you are.'** At least now, she seems to recognise that she has a duty to ask about Leon rather than just think about herself. She asks him questions about his life, and says she remembered his birthday but has forgotten his present. Leon explains how he's living with Maureen and Sylvia, and Carol changes the topic saying that she never comes to this part of Bristol as '**Rivers make me think about dying.'**

She says that she has something to tell Leon- **'I can't look after you properly, you know that, don't you?'** Leon keeps asking '**Why not?'** then worries that no one is looking after her. He says she could come and live with Maureen with him. Carol lashes back, saying '**Me? With her?'** and then **'I don't need a foster family. Is that what you think, that I need to go into care or go into a hospital, is that what you think, that I'm sick or incapable, is that what people say about me?'** She is clearly defensive, and reacting to what other people have advised her to do in the past. She starts shaking.

Maureen comes over to check on her, and Carol says she's being telling him '**what we agreed'**- that she can't be with him so he needs to stop running away. She says Leon can visit her whenever he likes, as long as she has enough notice. She says she has to get back, and shakes Maureen's hand. She kisses Leon and walks away. Leon watches her, and then runs after her, hugging from behind- **'she seems to go from hard to soft without moving a muscle.'** Leon asks if she still loves '**him',** meaning Jake. Carol says **'And you [...] I still love you.'** She walks away, curtsying before she goes. This is a contrast to the other times Leon has seen Carol- in Chapter 24 when Leon saw her at the family centre, he pretended to be Jake, and in Chapter 14 he gave her the picture of Jake. This is the first time we've seen her recognise that Leon is also her son.

For the rest of the day, they go on the battleship and eat lots of treats- so many Leon's teeth hurt. Maureen says she has something to tell him, and that is '**You're staying with me.**' Leon asks if it will be at the seaside, and Maureen says '**I'll tell you what the danger is in hearing half a conversation [...] You're likely to jump to conclusions.**' Maureen explains that no one is going to the seaside, and no one is getting a dog, '**for the tenth time.**' Her frustrated phrasing makes us think they've had a similar conversation before.

Maureen looks like she's going to cry, and '**he's sick of ladies crying all the time.**' However, she winks at him, and explains how she once broke her arm and had plaster on, and the plaster was itchy and she couldn't scratch it and she wasn't able to explore. She then explains that was an anecdote (albeit a bad one!) about how '**This isn't the whole of your life, love. This is a bit of your life.**' This reminds us of Sylvia's message in Chapter 25- '**We all have adventures, some are good and some are not so good.**' They are both trying to communicate to Leon that although things seem desperate now, they will get better.

She talks about how she's been arranging with social services to make things permanent, but she needs two promises from Leon- '**One, [...] you have to tell me when something's wrong. [...] Second, don't run away.**' Leon agrees, and Maureen says no more treats for a week.

Questions

1. How does Maureen's anecdote provide an effective metaphor for Leon's experiences?
2. How has Carol's character changed in this chapter?
3. In what ways is Carol's goodbye a pivotal moment in Leon's life?
4. What clues do you get in the chapter that the book is coming to a resolution?

Chapter 42

Summary

- It's the morning of the Royal Wedding, and Devlin arrives to help set things up. It quickly becomes evident that he and Sylvia are in a relationship.
- The celebrations are set up in the allotment, and as most people watch the wedding from their homes, Devlin, Tufty and Leon stay behind. Devlin and Tufty are now friends.
- Leon goes to water his plants, and looks down at the seeds remembering Jake. There is a sense of peace and hope.
- Maureen calls for Leon to come and help.

Analysis

It's the morning of the Royal Wedding, and Devlin comes to the house early to see Sylvia. She's still in bed, and swears before saying she needs 10 minutes to get ready. Devlin says **'She is not my queen, he is not my prince. I don't believe in royal anything.'** When Leon asks why, Devlin says he needs coffee first. Lots of people from Ireland are anti-royalist, because of the history of British Imperialism. The backdrop of the royal wedding could be significant- this was a day when many people celebrated what they called a 'fairy-tale wedding', but Charles and Diana's marriage later ended up in divorce and Diana later died at a young age in tragic circumstances. Although it seems like a happy backdrop for the final scene, there is a certain amount of irony for a modern reader who knows how this turns out. Is de Waal hinting that life for Leon won't be as good as it seems in this chapter? De Waal has said that she is planning on writing a sequel to the novel with Leon as an adult, and she hints that his life has not been easy.

Devlin is realistic about the wedding, and when Leon asks why he is coming he says because he was invited, and nods at Sylvia. She pre-emptively tells Devlin not to tell her off for her cigarette. Devlin has changed- he **'is clean these days and has found some other clothes.'** It turns out that he and Sylvia are seeing each other- **'all he does these days is look at Sylvia and she keeps saying what he thinks about things.'** This is a nice satisfactory ending for Sylvia who has always been despondent about her love life.

Devlin starts to prepare things, saying the Atwals (from the allotment) are bringing the tables, and he needs the bunting. Maureen comes in with some new slippers from Leon, and Devlin explains he got the money by helping clear at the allotment. Maureen says **'Didn't realise I was moving into a house of conspirators'**. However, she's teasing, and says Devlin has **'got [Sylvia] like a sixteen-year old.'** They both giggle. The atmosphere is light-hearted and pleasant.

At the allotments, Leon is ordered around to do lots of jobs. At the time of the wedding, everyone apart from Leon, Tufty and Devlin go to watch it inside. They sit at the allotments, and **'Leon likes it when they pretend to argue like they used to.'** We can see they're now good friends. The choice of setting for the Royal Wedding celebrations is significant- it is in the allotment, and we can see the two lives that Leon has struggled to keep separate coming together.

Devlin reminds Leon to water his plants, and he looks at the progress of his allotment and how the plants have grown. He opens a pod and looks at the seeds, and thinks **'It's strange to think that this little black bean will grow up to be a big plant and that plant will have its own seeds to make another plant and another seed and this will go on, over and over, for years, and he remembers what Maureen said about Jake. He hasn't gone forever.'** This image is a positive one, and will surely resonate with a reader. Leon has settled, and put down literal and metaphorical roots- he will no longer have to try to run away as he is happy and secure where he is. This is a moment of peace, contrasting to his anger and outbursts of before, and we hope that Leon can continue to settle and develop his own roots.

He then picks up his take-a-chance seeds, and says **'They are small and brown with wrinkled skin and nobody knows what's inside. He places them carefully in the soil and covers them over. He'll water than and look after them and hope for the best.'** This seems to be a metaphor about growing up- we never know what a child will turn out like, but if we nurture them and look after them, we hope that they can turn into great people in their own right.

The novel ends with Maureen calling for Leon, and him saying **'Coming.'** Not everything has a resolution in the novel- we want to know if Leon ever sees Jake again and how he grows up- but it is an optimistic and hopeful ending for Leon's future, as he starts to grow into an adult.

Although this is called a <u>coming-of-age</u> novel, it is interesting that Leon is only 10 when the novel ends- he has grown spiritually and emotionally, but is not 'of-age' yet.

Questions

1. Do you think this is a satisfactory ending to the novel? Are there any frustrating elements to it?
2. Do you think that the final chapter hints that Leon will have a happy rest of his life?
3. What do you think the message of the final chapter seems to be? Is there a central idea you think the author wanted us to be left with?
4. Do you think this is a coming-of-age novel?
5. What is the significance of the royal wedding being the backdrop to the final chapter?

Essay Hint- Conclusions

One thing to consider in a conclusion is the writer's intention- why did they write about the theme / character / concept in the question in the way they did? What does their message seem to be? Remember to be tentative because we don't know their exact intention, but can make inferences.

For example, if you had a question such as: **'To what extent is *My Name is Leon* an optimistic story?'** your conclusion might be something like:

In conclusion, it seems to be evident that although there are moments of sadness and despair, the overall message of the book is one of hope and optimism. Kit de Waal seems to be emphasising that there will be times in everyone's lives where things aren't positive, but these are just moments- like Leon, we will have to grow and adapt to overcome these obstacles. In that way, <u>My Name is Leon</u> seems to be a book of realistic optimism, accepting the bad parts of life but hoping things get better.

B – Contexts and Concepts

Biographical Context: Kit de Waal

Without Warning and Only Sometimes: Scenes from an Unpredictable Childhood

Kit de Waal has written memoirs of her childhood, which are interesting to read alongside *My Name is Leon* as you can see why she has chosen to write about some of these ideas and concepts.

De Waal lived in Birmingham in the 60s and 70s. Her mother was white and Irish, and her father was black and Jamaican. She writes about her experiences of growing up as one of the few biracial families in Birmingham, and how her family never really seemed to fit into either culture. Some of the chapter titles of her memoirs- 'I'm not living next to blackies' and 'The Irish are like that'- reflect the prejudice she faced growing up.

Like Leon, Kit de Waal did not have a conventional childhood. Her mother worked numerous jobs at once to try to make enough money to look after her children, including being a childminder and foster carer. She later converted to be a Jehovah's Witness, and de Waal's life changed significantly because of this. The title of her memoir- *Without Warning and Only Sometimes*- emphasises the unpredictability of her life growing up, something we also see reflected in *My Name is Leon*.

Later in her life, de Waal worked in criminal and family law, and became an expert in foster care including magistrate work, sitting on adoption panels, and writing training manuals on adoption and foster care.

De Waal spoke about her choice to write in close third person point of view, saying 'I have worked with lots of children in foster care, and so often their story is told by a social worker or their parent, or a foster carer or a guardian, anyone but the child. Even when social workers do their very best, it's not the same as hearing it from a child.'

My Name is Leon was her first published book, and she has written another full length novel, *The Trick to Time*, and a series of short stories about characters in her novels, *Supporting Cast* which includes short vignettes about characters including Wobbly Bobby, Sylvia, and Devlin. She has also written a Young Adult novel, *Becoming Dinah*.

Questions

1. What influences can you see from Kit de Waal's biographical information in the novel?
2. How important do you think it is to explore an author's life to understand a text?
3. Kit de Waal has announced that she plans to write a sequel to *My Name is Leon*. How does this make you feel?
4. De Waal promotes diversity in literature, and his established initiatives to support writers from underrepresented backgrounds. How does her commitment to diversity align with the themes of the novel?
5. De Waal also believes in the power of the working class, saying 'What a force we would be for change if we could all get together, speak with one voice, and overturn some of the terrible injustices that are going on.' What ideas about the working class does she explore in *My Name is Leon*?

Racial Tensions

Key Chapters: 20, 22, 23, 27, 29, 31, 33, 36, 39, 40

> 'We are not a warrior
> We are Africans by birth
> We have truth and rights and God besides
> We have dignity and worth.
>
> We have lost the way we used to live
> And the way that we behaved
> We are the consequence of history
> We are the warriors you made.'

In *My Name is Leon*, we can see lots of tension between the black community and other races. To understand this properly, we need to think about the history of black people in Britain.

Historical Background
Windrush Generation
After WWII, there was a huge shortage of people to work- a post-war labour shortage. Britain requested workers from other countries including the Carribean (which was part of the British Commonwealth), offering them British Citizenship and the right to work and live in the UK. The boat HMT Empire Windrush brought large groups of people to Britain between 1948 and 1973, and many of these workers took up jobs in the NHS and other sectors.

Most of the black and Asian population in Birmingham today are descendants of those who migrated to Britain in the post-war period. However, despite doing jobs that many people indigenous to Britain did not want to do, there was huge prejudice, and most could only find accommodation in neglected urban areas like Sparkbrook and Handsworth.

1960s
Tensions continued to grow. In 1964, Birmingham Conservative Candidate Peter Griffiths refused to condemn a racist slogan. In 1968, another politician Enoch Powell (who, ironically, had previously welcomed Caribbean nurses into Britain) gave his famous 'Rivers of

Blood' speech, where he called for migrants to be sent back to Barbados.

1970s

In the 1970s, race and immigration continued to be politicised, resulting in prejudice particularly against black and Asian communities. This led to a growth in resistance, and Britain saw lots of strikes in factories with those in low-skilled and low-paid jobs.

1980s- Uprisings

During the 80s, there was a recession, and struggles were not just limited to the workplace. There were a number of riots and protests against police brutality and systemic racism. The National Front were also a group of typically white British people who wanted non-white people to leave Britain, and a number of attacks on places of black and Asian celebration were committed in their name. It is important to note that these views were not universally shared, and many individuals and organisations were advocating for equality.

The following are some of the key events that led to racial tension and uprising in the 1980s:

- **January 1981 New Cross Road Fire**- after firebombs nearby at The Albany and Moonshot Club (typically frequented by black people) in preceding months, there was a birthday party in a private residence on New Cross Road. Witnesses saw a man throwing a petrol bomb in the window, but other evidence suggested it was set from inside the house, and the media villainised the people in the house. The fire led to the deaths of 13 young black people and injuries of many more. This fire became a symbol of the suffering and mistreatment many black people felt.
- **March 1981 Black People's Day of Action-** Thousands of people came to the streets of London to protest the mishandling of the New Cross Road Fire by police and the media.
- **April 1981 Operation Swamp-** After Margaret Thatcher's comment, 'The British people might be afraid of being swamped by people of a different culture', many black people were stopped and searched by the police, leading to further discontentment. Because of this, many people protested

against the treatment, leading to 3 days of fires, protests, and battles.
- **July 1981 Toxteth Liverpool-** after the arrest of Leroy Alphonse Cooper, on top of years of poverty and unfair treatment, there were 9 days of civil unrest with over 500 people arrested and 468 police injured. This was the first use of CS gas on crowds of people.
- **July 1981 Manchester-** similar tensions led to 2 days of unrest
- **10 July 1981 Birmingham Handsworth Uprising-** social deprivation and police harassment incited by sus laws (where police could stop and search anyone they believed looked suspicious, leading to an disproportionate number of black and Asian men being stopped) led to unrest and disturbances. A reported 40% of black youth had been stopped and searched in the previous year. Rumours of a National Front March led to 2 days of protest and uprising.
- **Further protests** characterised the rest of 1981, and there was another uprising in 1985 in Handsworth.

These tensions create the backdrop of *My Name is Leon,* and emphasise not only the struggles and hardships, but the resilience of an oppressed group of people. We can see different views on how to fight against oppression in the novel, and can see that that many people felt like protest was the only thing that would make people listen and incite change, for example: the argument between Castro, Mr Johnson and Tufty in Chapter 20 ('**Leon can hear that the others don't like Castro's army idea, but they don't like Mr Johnson's lobby idea either'**) ; the frustrations of Tufty in Chapter 27; the 'Ode to Castro' poem in Chapter 33; the conversation between Devlin and Tufty in Chapter 36.

Amnesty International, a human rights group, fights for the right of people across the world to protest. They argue: 'Protest is an invaluable way to speak truth to power. Throughout history, protests have been the driving force behind some of the most powerful social movements, exposing injustice and abuse, demanding accountability and inspiring people to keep hoping for a better future.'[3]

Historically, the protests led to greater media coverage of the struggles

---

[3] https://www.amnesty.org/en/what-we-do/freedom-of-expression/protest/

of an oppressed group, and incited discussion and change for a fairer society. However, there has been much in the media recently about unfair treatment, for example the police brutality and systemic racism that led to the deaths of Eric Garner, Ahmaud Arbery, and George Floyd to name a few. 2020 saw a new rise of Black Lives Matter Protests, showing the reader that these issues are still not resolved.

Black Role Models

In *My Name is Leon*, Tufty has a number of posters in his shed, which could allude to Martin Luther King (a human rights activist who fought for equality between black and white people), King Tufty (an influential Jamaican musician), and the 1968 Black Power Salute (a peaceful protest at the 1968 Olympics). See the information on Page 44 for more details.

Questions

1. The novel is set against a backdrop of racial tensions and riots in 1980s Britain. How does the author incorporate this into the narrative, and to what extent does it affect Leon's experiences?
2. How does Leon's mixed-race background affect his sense of identity in the story? At what point does he begin to explore his West Indian heritage?
3. Where does Leon experience racism in the novel? How does this affect how he perceives the world?
4. How does Leon's experience of the foster care system highlight issues about race in social care? Consider the different treatment of Leon and Jake.

Attitudes towards the Irish 🚩

Key chapters: 17, 24, 31, 36

> "'That's what you do, isn't it? You and your IRA. It's a protest. Get it? A protest. Except we don't bomb people in their beds like you Irish people.'
> 'Oh, every Irishman is a terrorist, is that what you're saying?'"

Kit de Waal's Irish Background

Kit de Waal is a national of both England and Ireland: her mother (Sheila O'Loughlin) was from Ireland. In her memoirs, *Without Warning and Only Sometimes,* de Waal has a chapter called 'The Irish are like that'. In this chapter, she describes how she hid her Irish heritage because of negative stereotypes because of the IRA. She describes how one girl at school said, '**My mom says the Irish are like that. They just want to kill us all. They're murderers and they don't care who they hurt.**' She describes the negative news coverage in the press, and how '**every day the Irish are worse than the day before – terrorists, murderers, evil, stupid.**'

> One of the key themes of the text is prejudice, and we can see through Tufty's treatment of Devlin (Chapters 17 and 36) that the Irish were negatively stereotyped. *My Name is Leon* explores the dangers of these stereotypes.

Stereotypes

The Irish were often portrayed in the media as drunk, lazy, and violent. This was historic, but saw a resurgence due to further immigration from Ireland and the news coverage of the IRA.

Irish Republican Army and The Troubles

The original IRA formed to seek an Independent Irish state, away from the rule of Britian. In the late 60s, the Provisional IRA were formed, who opposed to British forces in Northern Ireland. When people refer to the IRA, they often mean the Provisional IRA.

'The Troubles' refers to a period of conflict between the 1960s and 1990s, where the IRA responded to British forces and civilians with paramilitary violence, bombings, assassinations, and political strife.

By the late 1990s, the group and the British government came to a compromise, and the Good Friday Agreement of 1998 meant that the IRA was able to be disbanded.

1981 Irish Hunger Strikes

> In *My Name Is Leon*, there are several allusions to the 1981 Hunger Strikes. This links to the wider underlying theme of protest and rebellion. Set in 1980s Birmingham, we see frequent attempts to protest in the race riots and the links to the hunger strikes. Tufty's character refuses to engage in protest, preferring to '**accept. Let go. Breathe easy.**' Castro's character wants to create an '**army**' to fight, whereas Mr Johnson wants to '**organise**' and '**lobby.**'
>
> All of these characters, and the background of the Hunger Strikes, force the reader to consider the ethics of protest, and how and when we should stand up for our beliefs.

The 1981 Irish Hunger Strikes were part of the political conflict between Irish nationalists (who were seeking independence from Britain) and the British government. The hunger strikes were mainly led by members of the Provisional Irish Republican Army (IRA) who were imprisoned in the Maze Prison / Long Kesh.

Special Category Status had allowed IRA prisoners to be treated as political prisoners, giving them certain privileges and distinguishing them from common criminals. However, the British government ended this status in 1976, leading to protests and dissatisfaction among Republican prisoners. As a form of protest, the prisoners refused to wear the prison clothes and instead went naked with a blanket, which they called 'On the blanket'. They demanded that they be reissued their status as political prisoners and the privileges these afforded.

When this didn't work, a prisoner called Bobby Sands led a hunger strike with 9 others. Many communities rallied together to support these strikes, in Ireland and across the world. There were rallies, protests, and solidarity acts with significant media publicity.

However, the British government (led by Margaret Thatcher, the Prime Minister of the time) refused to meet the prisoners' demands. They portrayed the hunger strike as a criminal act rather than a political protest.

Despite being in prison, Bobby Sands was elected as a Member of Parliament for the Fermanagh and South Tyrone constituency while on hunger strike. Despite this, the British Government still refused to meet the demands of the prisoners.

Despite efforts by the families, the Catholic Church, and others to find a resolution, Bobby Sands and the nine other hunger strikers died between May and August 1981. Their deaths resulted in increased tension and unrest within Northern Ireland, with petrol bombs being thrown at the police and armies, and other demonstrations.

While the hunger strikes did not immediately achieve their goals, they contributed to the eventual political negotiations and peace process that led to the Good Friday Agreement in 1998, which helped bring an end to the Troubles and established a framework for peace and governance in Northern Ireland.

Questions

1. Consider Leon's relationship with Devlin. How does their friendship challenge societal norms and expectations?
2. Do you think that Tufty and Devlin are racist towards one another in the novel? Is this surprising?

Cultural References

There are many allusions to cultural refences in the novel that you may not be familiar with. Understanding them, and how they contribute to themes and concepts, is important.

The Dukes of Hazzard
- This was a TV show about two brothers who race around in a car trying to escape the law, and their various escapades.
- The show is mentioned 7 times in the novel, and Leon even wants to call Jake 'Bo' after one of the characters. Near the end of the novel, it's referenced as Leon is trying to get away from Tufty and Devlin, as he remembers where to keep his weapon pointed.
- This motif appeals to Leon's sense of adventure, but also his desire for his family to stick together.

Action Men
- Action Men are mentioned 21 times in the novel; they are Leon's favourite toy, and it reminds the reader of Leon's youth (despite his often mature sounding observations)
- Leon often dreams he's a soldier- like Action Man- and this motif highlights his protective instincts. This is also highlighted when Leon has to move to Maureen's house, and leaves one of the action men behind to make room for Jake's toys; he is selfless (although he laments this selfless act later in the novel!)

Phone Boxes
- In the 80s, working class people did not usually have phones in their homes; they had to go to a phone box in the street.
- Near the start of the novel, Carol often leaves her sons to go to the phone box to call Tony. This perhaps emphasises her isolation and desperation for connection and her negligence of her children.

The Royal Wedding of Charles and Diana
- Sylvia, like many people in the 80s, was obsessed with the wedding of Charles and Diana. Diana was known as the 'People's Princess' as she was more in touch with the everyday person than the traditional royals, and many people saw this as

a fairy-tale wedding. There were street parties (like Sylvia and her friends plan) which connected many people.
- Devlin shows an anti-royalist attitude in Chapter 42, saying '**It is not a fairy tale. It is a wedding.**' He demonstrates the views of people who were not as enchanted at the royal wedding as Sylvia was.
- However, the marriage later ended in divorce and a tragic death for Diana. Perhaps the reader senses the dramatic irony of the novel ending on a celebration of the wedding- everything does not turn out like the fairy-tale it seemed, maybe like Leon's life.

Margaret Thatcher
- Margaret Thatcher was the first female prime minister of the UK, and led the Conservative Party in 1979. She supported the free market and was anti-communist, so much so she was nicknamed 'The Iron Lady' because of her strong principles. However, she implemented a fixed tax and economic reforms which counteracted recession, but led to deindustrialisation, particularly of coal mines and steel mills, which led to mass unemployment. Together with her social welfare cuts and opposition to trade unions, she became particularly unpopular with the working classes.
- Maureen calls Margaret Thatcher a 'bloody cow' and says she can 'kiss her arse.' Margaret Thatcher created many policies about work and the economy which impacted unemployment rates, and had a negative impact particularly on the working class.

West Indian Cultural Identity
- **Reggae Music:** There are several references to Reggae music, particularly in Chapter 29 when Leon and Tufty listen to the Boom Box. Reggae artists had a significant role in cultural expression and community for the West Indian culture, and we can see the importance of the artform in establishing a sense of cultural identity.
- **Dominoes:** Both Tufty and Leon's father played domines in the West Indian way- loudly, exuberantly, and aggressively. We can see how people from the West Indian Culture bond together over these traditions and experiences.

Foster Care System
- Even nowadays, up to 40% of siblings are split up when they enter the social care system. In *My Name is Leon* we can see the negative consequences of this in terms of Leon's development and identity.
- Some of the social workers don't treat Leon like a person, or even look at him- Earring sees his visit as a tickbox exercise, and it's only the Zebra (who bring Leon his BMX- a symbol of freedom in the novel- and forces him to look at her when she speaks to him) who seems to be a good social worker.
- Kit de Waal seems to be using some of her own experiences to present ideas about social care and the inadequacies of the system, as well as acknowledging those who wish to do good and make a positive change for disadvantaged young people.

Questions

1. What motifs do you think are most important for exploring Leon's character and development?
2. If this novel was rewritten so it was set in the 2020s, what aspects do you think would be lost? What would different? What would be the same?
3. Why do you think de Waal chose this time period to set the book?

Essay Hint- Writing about context

The AQA Examiner's report from 2018 talks about how the most successful candidates 'incorporated AO3 into their responses and focused on linking their contextual points back to the question throughout their response, rather than bolting context onto the end.

You will not get marks for including things about context if it doesn't link to your argument and question, and it might actually lower your mark if it disrupts the clarity of your argument. Remember, AO3 talks about context AND concepts and ideas- if you're answering the questions properly, and considering what wider issues and ideas are being explored, you'll get marks for AO3.

Literary Influences and Genre

Coming-of-age / bildungsroman
Coming-of-age novels typically explore the spiritual / moral development as a child coming into adulthood. Generally, they contain themes about identity, losing innocence, and accepting that life is not going to be perfect.

My Name is Leon fits much of this, and is about Leon growing up and accepting parts of his life, much like the ongoing metaphor of the allotment and the plants growing. However, at the end of the novel, Leon is still only 10 and perhaps still holds onto the hope that he will someday rescue Jake.

Other coming of age novels include *The Perks of Being a Wallflower* by Stephen Chbosky, *All the Bright Places* by Jennifer Niven, and *Simon vs the Homo Sapiens Agenda* by Becky Albertalli.

Social Realism
Social Realism novels want to depict ordinary lives of ordinary people, and address social issues that many people face. Kit de Waal has said that she wants to champion the working classes and give a voice to those who are not often given a voice. Other social realist novels include most works by Charles Dickens, Emile Zola, and John Green.

My Name is Leon explores the realities of life for children in the foster system, those with mental health struggles, and the working class, and de Waal uses this genre to highlight social disparities and challenges.

Child Narrators and Perspectives
As a reader, we are offered an intimate view into Leon's thoughts and perspectives, and can view situations as he does. Other novels which do this include *The Curious Incident of the Dog in the Night Time* by Mark Haddon (another GCSE set text), *Life of Pi* by Yann Martel, and *To Kill a Mockingbird* by Harper Lee.

Historical Fiction
Set in the 80s, *My Name is Leon* follows a tradition of novels being set in a notable period in history. In a time period defined by social dissatisfaction, *My Name is Leon* uses the backdrop of the 80s to

explore key themes and ideas. It is important to note that the characters are fictional, and some events are fictional, such as Castro's death leading to the uprising in the latter chapters.

Notable Young Adult historical fiction includes *Salt to the Sea* by Ruta Sepetys and *Outrun the Moon* by Stacey Lee.

Own Voices and Identity-Centric Literature
Kit de Waal has demonstrated commitment to representing marginalised voices, and *My Name is Leon* contributes to this movement by sharing experiences which align to de Waal's own identity. Books like *Long Way Day* by Jason Reynolds and *The Hate U Give* by Angie Thomas also fall into these traditions.

Questions

1. What other books have you read that are similar to *My Name is Leon*? What did you enjoy about both those novels?
2. Do you think that *My Name is Leon* can be characterised as a coming-of-age novel?

Essay Hint- Discussing Genre

Don't just add the genre of the text in if you're not going to talk about it! Have a look at how the following sentences link the genre into discussion of a theme.

A question about identity:

As a coming-of-age novel, which typically explores themes of identity and development, My Name is Leon explores various factors that can contribute to a child developing their own identity, such as family, role models, and popular culture.

A question about protest:

De Waal uses the genre of historical fiction to establish the setting of the story in 1980s Birmingham, a time characterised by protests, uprising, and social change.

C – Character Profiles

Character List

This list is alphabetised. You can refer to it if you need a reminder about who a character is. Characters with asterixis have full character profiles later in the guide.

Alan: Carol's boyfriend with a sports car, who drops her off in Chapter 14 to see Leon at Maureen's.

Atwals: An Indian couple who have a plot at the allotments.

Byron Francis: Leon's father. He often visited Carol in Leon's childhood, but was sentenced to prison for an undisclosed crime. Although he treats Leon well, there are suggestions that he is violent, such as how he threatened a neighbour's dog in Chapter 4 and verbally abusive to Carol as he calls her crazy in Chapter 7.

Carol Rycroft:* Leon and Jake's mum. She has mental health problems, and after Leon and Jake are taken away from her she spends time in different institutions.

Castro: One of Tufty's friends. He wants to instigate change in terms of how black people are treated, and believes an 'army' is needed. He gives his views on this in Chapter 20, is arrested in Chapter 27, and hides in Tufty's shed in Chapter 31. He is killed by police, and is what prompts the uprising and protest at the end of the book. His name is used in Tufty's Ode in Chapter 33.

Devlin / Victor Devlin: An old Irish man who works at the allotments. Leon also hangs around him, but seems more wary of him. There are numerous hints to his past, but it turns out he is a man who is grieving his dead son. He seems to be going out with Sylvia at the end of the novel.

Earring: A social worker only seen in Chapter 28. His questions seem to be a tick boxing exercise, and Leon recognises that he doesn't care about him. Leon imagines stabbing him with a pen.

Jake: Leon's brother. He is initially fostered by Maureen in Chapter 6 in a temporary placement, but is adopted in Chapter 10 by a family who the other side of Birmingham.

Leon:* The <u>protagonist</u> of the novel.

Martin: Another foster child at Leon's school. He sometimes gets into fights. Only seen in Chapter 21.

Marvo, Waxy, and Stump: Tufty's black friends who play dominoes with him in Chapter 20.

Maureen:* The lady who fosters Leon and looks after him for the first half of the book. She is concerned about Leon eating enough, and has fostered lots of children before. She falls ill in Chapter 15, and only returns to look after Leon in Chapter 35.

Mr Johnson: Another one of Tufty's black friends we see in Chapter 20. He wants to organise black people to lobby for change, but his views are criticised by the other black people who want a different method to seek reform. Tufty works for Mr Johnson at a bike shop.

Rainbow: A black man the police are searching for in Chapter 27, as he is being accused of leading the early riot on Carpenter Road.

Salma / Sally: A social worker Leon sometimes calls Sally. She seems to be the one who facilitates the adoption of Jake, and in Chapter 12 she leaves her bag in the living room and Leon reads the files on his mum.

Sylvia: Maureen's sister. Initially, in Chapter 13 there seems to be a mutual dislike between Leon and Sylvia, but Sylvia agrees to look after him in Chapter 16 after Maureen is admitted to hospital, and her and Leon's relationship grows throughout the text.

Tina: Carol's neighbour at the start of the novel. She often looks after the children for Carol, although her boyfriend is sick of her doing it so much. She keeps an eye on Carol until they have a row about money, and she is the one to call social services.

Tony: Jake's father. He has a relationship with Carol when he is 39 and she is 25. It seems like he promised her a relationship and that he would leave his girlfriend and child for her, but later says they're over. We only see him in Chapter 4.

Tufty / Mr Burrows / Linwood Burrows / Wasp Man:* A black man who cycles and works at the allotments. Leon likes to hang around with him, and sees him as a role model.

Wobbly Bobby: Tina's child.

Woman in a flowery skirt: A lady who has the best allotments at Rookery Road.

The Zebra: The social worker who seems to be most caring towards Leon. She is the one who initially takes Leon and Jake from their home in Chapter 5, brings Leon a BMX in Chapter 16, and takes Leon to see Maureen in hospital in Chapter 19, and oversees the visit between Leon and Carol at the Family Centre in Chapter 24.

Questions

1. What role do you think nicknames have in the novel? Is there a difference between the nicknames that the black community use, the names people call Leon, and the names Leon gives to other characters?
2. Some characters have a huge focus on the first part of the book (for example, Tina and Tony), but aren't heard of again. What might this reflect about Leon's life?
3. In Kit de Waal's collection of short stories, 'Supporting Cast', she writes short vignettes about some of the characters in *My Name is Leon:* Carol Rycroft, Sylvia, Wobbly Bobby, Bryon Francis, Mr Devlin, The Zebra, Castro, and Woman in a Flowery Skirt. Which one of these would you most like to read, and why?

Leon

Leon's importance to the novel as a whole
Leon is the protagonist of the novel, and through de Waal's use of third person limited narrative voice, we see events and characters through his perspective. We see Leon's development and gradual acceptance of the situation he is in, and through his character we are forced to explore ideas about identity, family, and belonging.

Leon's key moments
Leon's life can be roughly divided into key sections:

Chapters 1-5: Jake is born. Carol struggles to cope with raising two children, and Leon gradually takes on more and more responsibility.

Chapters 6-10: Leon lives with Maureen and Jake in Maureen's house. Although Leon has bad dreams, he seems to be adjusting to life here.

Chapters 11-15: Jake is taken away to be adopted. Maureen and Leon seem to be less happy without him. Maureen gradually becomes more ill.

Chapters 16-19: Leon moves in to live with Sylvia whilst Maureen in hospital. He doesn't seem to enjoy his time with her, and spends as much time as he can going to the allotments to be with Tufty and Devlin.

Chapters 20-24: As Leon spends more time with Tufty, there is more of a focus on race and the first protest happens on Carpenter Road, turning into a riot.

Chapters 25-33: Leon is ill with flu in Chapter 25, and this seems to be a turning point in their relationship as she looks after him. We hear more about the oppression of black people, and the tensions between Castro and the police.

Chapters 34-39: Maureen returns. Leon overhears her and Sylvia fantasising about living by the sea, and decides to run away to collect Jake and then his mum to live in a shed at the allotment. He is seen by Tufty and Devlin, and runs away into the middle of a stand-off between police and protesters. The men rescue him.

Chapters 40-42: Leon returns to Sylvia's house with Devlin and Tufty. He sees his mum, and is given some closure. The novel ends with the royal wedding celebrations, and the adults he loves coming together.

Key Quotations:

'The empty sound in the house is louder than Jake crying for his bottle.' (Ch. 13) This quotation demonstrates Leon's intense love for Jake, and how much he misses him when he's gone. It is a mature recognition of the physical and emotional pain of missing someone, and the sensory imagery makes the reader feel sympathy for Leon. Because of Leon being forced to look after Jake from a young age, he feels a sense of responsibility for him. He misses Jake throughout the text, and his key aim is to get Jake back.
'You're nice and big for your age. A right little man.' (Ch. 1) From the very first chapter of the novel, Leon is recognised as being tall for his age. Throughout the novel, repeated reference is made to Leon's appearance, and that he seems a lot older than he is. Perhaps Leon is expected to respond to things in a more mature way than his 9/10 year old self because of his appearance.
'She squeezes his fingers and he can feel her love travelling all the way down from her heart into his. It's like special electricity, a secret.' (Ch. 14) Despite her flaws, Leon loves his mother. In this quotation, where Leon sees his mother at Maureen's house, we see that he recognises the love as something physical, and longs for connection. However, as a reader, we can recognise that Carol is not well enough to return that love. However, there is a sense of closure in the penultimate chapter of the book as Carol finally admits she loves Leon as well as Jake, and says it's time for him to move on.
'But out of all the social workers he's ever had, she looks at him the most.' (Ch. 16) Although there are many situations Leon misunderstands because of his age, there are some complexities he sees to grasp quickly, showing wisdom beyond his age. This quotation is one such instance- he seems to grasp that many of the social workers don't properly see or acknowledge him, and he recognises when people do care about him.

> 'If Leon had a remote control he would [...] turn Sylvia off, click, and the teachers off, click, and the social workers off, click, click, click. Then he would crush the remote control with a big hammer so they could never come on again.' (Ch. 21)

This quotation demonstrates anger towards the adults in his life. He feels frustrated at the lack of control he has in his situation, and sometimes his frustration comes out physically (for example, when he blocks Sylvia's toilet and wrecks his room at Maureen's), and sometimes we just see his emotional outbursts in his head like this. This quotation also highlights the power of the imagination.

> 'all the things he's collected' (Ch. 25)

The euphemism of a 'collection' shows that Leon sees the things he's stolen as something valuable. Later on, in Chapter 31 he says he 'doesn't want to spend any of his money on carrot seeds because he's going to need every penny.' We come to recognise that Leon steals for a number of reasons- firstly, to feel in control. Secondly, as a punishment for people who he sees doing wrong (like stealing Sylvia's back door key when she speaks badly about his mum). Thirdly, to 'collect' things that will able him to fulfil his fantasy of rescuing Jake and his mum, and supporting them.

> 'He smiles. Just like Maureen has a soft voice and Sylvia has three or four different voices, Leon can have a pretend voice as well.' (Ch. 35)

Here, after Leon has experienced what he believes is a betrayal from Maureen, he learns to lie. We have heard about him lying in the past in dialogue and snippets of conversation, but this is the first time Leon acknowledges lying himself.

> 'No one cares about me. No one cares about my brother. I've got a baby as well. He's my baby. [...] I can't see him. I keep asking and asking but you only care about yourself. Everyone steals things from me.' (Ch. 37)

This explosive quotation is a contrast to Leon's usual exchanges with Devlin and Tufty- he is generally quiet, or asking or answering questions. Here, he expresses his anger and hurt at how the adults in his life have been treating him, and about his circumstances in general. The snippet 'Everyone steals from me' is particularly emotive, perhaps justifying to the reader why Leon steals, as everything he cares about has been taken away from him.

'Leon holds his arms open. "We are not a warrior", he says. "We have dignity and worth."' (Ch. 39)

As Leon faces the police officer in Chapter 39, he quotes a line from Tufty's poem, 'Ode to Castro.' In his own way, Leon diffuses the situation with both childlike innocence but also understanding ahead of his years. This peaceful small moment of protest emphasises the power of poetry and communication.

'It's strange to think that this little black bean will grow up to be a big plant and that plant will have its own seeds to make another plant and another seed and this will go on, over and over, for years, and he remembers what Maureen said about Jake. He hasn't gone forever.' (Ch. 42)

This moment is a peaceful one at the end of the novel, and demonstrates Leon's current acceptance of the situation. He recognises, by using the metaphor of a seed, that situations grow and change; all we can do is make the best of the situations we are put into.

Writer's Methods
De Waal's use of third person limited narrator means that we hear the events from Leon's perspective. By using a child's perspective, de Waal evokes sympathy for Leon as we empathise with what he's going through. Frequent flashbacks and shifts in time means that we slowly learn more about Leon's past, and worry about his future.

Example AQA-style question about the character of Leon
How far does de Waal present Leon as a character who is able to cope with difficult circumstances?

Write about:
- What difficult circumstances Leon faces in the novel
- How de Waal presents Leon as coping with these circumstances

Carol

Carol's importance to the novel as a whole

As Leon's mother, Carol is influential in Leon's ***formative*** *(early)* years. Her **'itinerant lifestyle'** and **'emotionally unstable personality disorder'** means she is not capable of looking after her children, or at times herself. She seems to have unstable relationships with men, and appears to be reluctant or unable to see Leon after he is fostered. This leads to significant stress and trauma for Leon. At the end of the novel, however, there is a key moment of reconciliation where Carol says she loves Leon, which creates an effective <u>resolution</u>.

Carol's key moments

Chapter 1: Jake is born. Carol goes for a cigarette instead of feeding him, and relies on her neighbour Tina to look after Leon.

Chapter 2: We get more hints that Carol struggles to cope with raising two children, and Leon gradually takes on more and more responsibility. She keeps Leon home from school to help, ironically while telling him the importance of getting a good education.

Chapter 3: Carol is crying more and more, and in a conversation overheard by Leon we learn more about her relationship with Tony.

Chapter 4: Tony arrives to tell Carol to stop trying to contact him- their relationship is over. She shouts at Leon for being seen by Tony, but later tells him he has to look after himself and Jake, and '**get something more out of life.**'

Chapter 5: Carol gradually moves to a catatonic state, wetting herself in her bed and not moving. When Tina sees, she calls social services.

Chapter 7: Leon has a memory of Carol and Byron fighting over Jake, and his mother then crying.

Chapter 12: Leon reads Salma's file about his mum, and we learn about her personality disorder, addictions, and institutions she's been in.

Chapter 14: Carol visits Leon at Maureen's house. She crumples to the floor after seeing a picture of Jake, and asks for the photo. She does not ask much about Leon.

Chapter 24: Carol visits Leon at the family centre. She looks more ill, and breaks down banging her head on the wall. Leon pretends he's Jake to calm her down.

Chapter 41: Leon visits Carol in Bristol. She explains she's unable to look after Leon, and he stop running away. Leon asks if she still loves Jake, and she replies that she loves Leon too.

Key Quotations

> 'Can I do it in a minute? Sorry, I was just going to the smoking room.' (Ch. 1)

From the first chapter, we can see Carol putting her own needs before her children's when she's asked by the nurse to feed Jake. Her proclivity for addiction is foreshadowed with her need for cigarettes, and the irony of her doing something so linked to disease and death after just giving birth is highlighted.

> 'Just me and you and him. Always.' (Ch. 1)

This quotation demonstrates that Carol does care for Leon and Jake, and has good intentions. Perhaps de Waal is commenting on the poor state of the health services in the 80s, which failed to support someone who had struggled with post-natal depression and had to have her first child temporarily fostered before. There is also an irony to this quotation, as the reader will probably know from the blurb that they will not always be together.

> 'Carol used to say sorry when she shouted at him but she forgets all the time these days so tomorrow he's going to take some money out of her purse.' (Ch. 4)

After swearing and shouting at Leon after Tony saw him, Carol does not apologise. Here we can see how her actions and the unfairness Leon feels trigger his stealing. We feel sympathy for Leon here, and concern about the comment that 'she forgets all the time', especially when she has been forgetting other things essential to looking after her children.

> 'He realizes that the whole room smells like Jake's nappy and that his mum has wet the bed again. He opens the window but only a little crack in case Carol gets cold.' (Ch. 5)

At this point in the text, we realise the extent of Carol's illness- the chapter began saying 'things get jangled up at home', but this moment emphasises how much of an understatement that was. The single word 'again' highlights how this isn't just a one-off, but has been going on for an extended time. Carol's inability to look after her children or herself is juxtaposed by Leon's inherently caring nature, as he is concerned about her feeling cold.

'**Itinerant lifestyle**' and '**emotionally unstable personality disorder**.' (Ch. 12)
We learn a bit more about Carol's mental health struggles through the files in Salma's purse: Carol is dependent on alcohol and prescription drugs, and isn't capable of looking after her children. De Waal could be making the reader consider the support that those with mental health problems receive, particularly in the 1980s. Despite Carol having previous history of post-natal depression leading to Leon's previous stay in temporary foster homes, there seems to be little if no support for her after Jake's birth. This makes the reader feel empathy for Carol, and we recognise it is not her fault, but responsibility needs to lie with support services as well.
'**He feels a dark star of pain in his throat and the last warmth of her touch on his fingers.**' (Ch. 14)
The metaphor of 'a dark star of pain' is almost oxymoronic; 'star' is positive, but 'dark' and 'pain' have negative connotations. This is almost symbolic of their relationship, as Leon looks up to Carol and admires her, as she is his biological mother, but Carol's mental health issues mean she is not able to look after Leon, causing him hurt and pain.
'**he doesn't see her turn around and wave because she didn't.**' (Ch. 25)
This is another heart-breaking moment in the novel. After Carol's visit in Chapter 24 at the family centre, she doesn't turn and wave. Leon can't seem to get over the fact that she wouldn't want to turn around and see him for one last time.
'**she seems to go from hard to soft without moving a muscle. […] "And you […] I still love you."**' (Ch. 41)
This is a key turning point in the novel, and presents a satisfying resolution for the reader. Knowing that his mum doesn't need rescuing, and accepting that he is loved although she's not able to be with him is a key moment in Leon's development, and in the final chapter we see him beginning his journey into acceptance.

Writer's Methods
De Waal uses Carol, Leon's biological mother, to contrast against the other maternal figures (Sylvia and Maureen) in Leon's life to question what makes a good mother. The character is also used as a commentary on mental health, and support for those who are struggling.

AQA Style questions about the character of Carol
How does de Waal present Leon's relationship with Carol?

Write about:
- Leon's feelings towards his mother and how his mother behaves towards him
- How de Waal presents the relationship between Leon and his mother

How does de Waal present ideas about what makes a good mother?

Write about:
- The mother figures in Leon's life, and how they help to nurture him.
- How de Waal presents ideas about what makes a good mother.

Maureen

Maureen's importance to the novel as a whole
As Leon's foster mother (first temporary, and then permanent at the end of the novel), Maureen is important as a foil character to Carol, Leon's biological mother. She juxtaposes Carol in the ways she is nurturing and knows how to best support Leon (and Jake's) social, emotional, and physical development.

Maureen's key moments

Chapter 6: Leon and Jake's first day at Maureen's. We immediately see the contrast between the *maternal (motherly)* characters.

Chapter 7: Maureen looks after Leon when he can't sleep at night. Further contrasts are established between Carol and Maureen.

Chapter 9: Six months into their living together, we see more of the normalised relationship between Maureen and Leon.

Chapter 10: Maureen deals with the fall out of Leon realising Jake is going to be adopted.

Chapter 11: Maureen supports Leon as he struggles to cope with Jake's absence.

Chapter 13: Maureen takes Jake to Sylvia's house. The reader sees her ill health clearly for the first time.

Chapter 14: As Carol visits, we see the contrast between the characters first time. We recognise Maureen's dislike of Carol.

Chapter 15: Maureen is taken into hospital with '**bronchial pneumonia.**'

Chapter 16: Leon visits Maureen in hospital and realises how frail she is.

Chapter 35: Maureen returns home. She and Sylvia fantasise about living somewhere by the sea, and Leon thinks they intend to abandon him as well. He feels betrayed, which is the catalyst for his running away.

Chapter 40: Maureen is angry and upset when Leon comes home from the riot, but eventually Leon recognises it was just her fear that made her angry.

Chapter 41: Maureen takes Leon to see Carol in Bristol, and we get a sense of closure. She explains that everyone has good and bad moments in life.

Chapter 42: In the final chapter of the novel, Leon remembers Maureen's promise that Jake hasn't gone forever.

Key Quotations

> 'her fuzzy red hairstyle looks like a flaming halo.' (Ch. 6)

This simile compares Maureen to an angel, and implies to the reader that Maureen will be a saviour-type character to Leon. From the first chapter we see her, she is connected with passion (the 'flam[e]' of the halo might represent her fierce love) and healing.

> 'I'll keep saying it until you believe me, Leon. You will be all right and that, mister, is a promise.' (Chapter 11)

Maureen's reassuring tone here shows how much she empathises with Leon and wants to support him. However, she promises him things which she cannot know are true, and perhaps Leon senses the dishonesty in this.

> 'Er, no, Carol. No, you cannot. [...] He hasn't got much else, has he? He's not at home with you where he should be and he hasn't got his brother, which he's finding bloody hard if you don't mind me saying.' (Chapter 14)

Maureen's frustration with Carol is evident here as she snaps when Carol wants to take the picture of Jake for herself. Although Maureen tries to keep her negative thoughts about Carol to herself, when seeing Carol's self-centred nature first hand, it comes out.

> 'She smells different, she looks different and she sounds different, but when she snuggles him and rubs his back she is the same.' (Ch. 19)

Leon recognises here the frailty of Maureen- she is ill and in hospital, and no longer able to look after him. The anaphora of 'she' and a sense emphasises the contrast between Maureen before and after the illness. However, the unconditional nature of their love is revealed with the power of her hugging him.

> 'deep in his brain, he can hear something screaming and wailing, the new realisation that Maureen is just like everyone else. [...] He smiles. Just like Maureen has a soft voice and Sylvia has three or four different voices, Leon can have a pretend voice as well.' (Ch. 35)

Here, Leon thinks that Maureen plans to abandon him to go with Sylvia to the seaside. This is the catalyst for him running away- the person he felt like he could depend on most in the world has seemingly betrayed him. The motif of the 'pretend voice' emerges again, but this time, it's Leon who has learnt to lie and cover up his emotions. This is a key turning point in the bildungsroman.

'**Have you had a wee? You'll need a sandwich before bed. Bet you're starving aren't you?' 'You're back. That's enough for now.'** (Chapter 40)

When Maureen is finally over her anger at Leon sneaking off, she reverts back to her old ways: checking Leon has had a wee and feeding him. We realise her anger was founded in upset and worry, and are relieved their relationship is beginning to get back to how it was.

'**This isn't the whole of your life, love. This is a bit of your life.**' (Ch. 41)

After seeing Carol, Maureen recognises that Leon is in a bad place in his life, but tries to be *pragmatic (realistic)* and acknowledge that sometimes we all go through bad periods in our life, and this is one of Leon's. This reminds us of Sylvia's statement in Chapter 25, that '**we all have adventures. Some are good, some are not so good.**' De Waal's story seems to be *didactic (teaching us a lesson):* we will all go through bad times, but they won't last. The ending is both optimistic and realistic.

Example AQA-style question about the character of Maureen

How does de Waal use Maureen to explore ideas about what makes a good parent in *My Name is Leon*?
Write about:
- Where Maureen is a good parent-figure in Leon's life
- How de Waal uses Maureen to explore ideas about what makes a good parent

Sylvia

Sylvia's Importance to the novel

As Maureen's sister, we see numerous juxtapositions between the siblings. Regardless, Sylvia turns out to be a character Leon can trust, despite his initial dislike of her. We see that Sylvia is fiercely loyal to those she loves, and though her parenting methods are unconventional, Leon grows to love and trust her. Despite being unmarried, Sylvia is a romantic at heart, spending time and effort planning a street party for the royal wedding. We see hints of her previously abusive past marriage, but the ending is happy as Sylvia and Devlin seem to be in a relationship.

Sylvia's Key Moments

Chapter 13: Leon and Maureen go around to Sylvia's house. We learn that Leon doesn't like Sylvia, and Sylvia doesn't like how much time and energy Maureen is expending on Leon.

Chapter 15: When Maureen is taken into hospital, Sylvia agrees to look after Leon as Leon's quick calling for the ambulance may have saved Maureen's life.

Chapter 25: Leon is ill, and Sylvia looks after him. This seems to be a turning point in their relationship.

Chapter 28: The Earring- a social worker who doesn't really seem to care- comes to speak to Leon. When Leon has a tantrum afterwards, Sylvia helps him to clean it up.

Chapter 29: Sylvia is acting distant, and Leon worries that she's angry at him.

Chapter 30: It's Leon's birthday, and Sylvia organises a tea party with her friends as she doesn't know any of Leon's.

Chapter 31: Still worried about Leon's lack of friends, Sylvia takes him to watch a film with a boy with special needs. Leon is embarrassed.

Chapter 32: Leon goes shopping with Sylvia. They share a private joke about a rabbit based on one of Sylvia's stories, but then Leon feels betrayed when he overhears her mentioning to a friend that she wants Maureen to stop fostering when she is out of hospital.

Chapter 34: Sylvia is excited because Maureen is coming home. However, the day before she goes on a date which doesn't end well. Leon comforts her.

Chapter 35: Maureen returns, and the sisters dream about a life at the seaside. Leon thinks they mean without him, which triggers his plan to run away and rescue Jake.
Chapter 40: When Leon comes back to the house after the riot, Sylvia looks after Devlin and dresses his wounds.
Chapter 42: It is evident that Sylvia and Devlin are in a relationship. They celebrate the Royal Wedding at the allotments, ans we see that the family seem to be happy.

'**Leon nods and Sylvia pokes him in the back. "You make bloody sure. If you don't and anything happens to her, you'll be sorry."'** (Ch. 13)
The first time we see Sylvia, the reader recognises that she doesn't know how to speak to children properly. Her tone with Leon is fierce and aggressive. On the other hand, we get a sense of her fierce loyalty and need to protect those she loves.
'**He's a good lad. He's saved her bloody life, he has. She always said he was a good kid, Mo did. I'll have him. Yes, I will. Bless him**.' (Ch. 15)
Juxtaposing Sylvia's attitude to Leon before in Chapter 13 (when she threatened him and refused to use his name), Sylvia responds to the belief that Leon saved Maureen with loyalty; she says she will foster him temporarily.
'**We all have adventures, some are good and some are not so good.**' (Ch. 25)
Leon wants Sylvia to tell him a story when he is ill, but Sylvia instead tells him a joke about a rabbit which Leon decides '**isn't a story, it's a trick.**' However, the moral Sylvia says comes from this story is pragmatic and insightful- not everything in life is good, but there may be better things that happen later. This foregrounds what Maureen says at the end of the novel that '**this is a bit of [Leon's] life'**, not the whole of it.
'**Don't s**t where you sit.**' (Ch. 28)
After the Earring's visit, Leon makes a mess in the bathroom, putting toilet roll and a dressing gown down the toilet. He wets himself in his anger. Sylvia helps him to clean it up, but in a way which contrasts

Maureen's more caring way- whereas Maureen let him eat ice cream after his tantrum in Chapter 10, Sylvia makes him clean up himself and then tells him this adage- crude for a young boy! Regardless, we see that Sylvia, in her own way, cares for Leon, and is giving him more boundaries than he perhaps had with Maureen.

'Sylvia and Leon both think of the rabbit story and smile at each other. Sylvia even checks his bum as they walk past.' (Ch. 32)

Since his illness, there is more friendship and comradery between Sylvia and Leon, and this private joke highlights this. The joke seems to summarise Sylvia well- it is slightly rude and inappropriate, but born out of when she looked after Leon when he was poorly.

'he holds her hand because that's what she did when he started crying when he was sick.' (Ch. 34)

This quotation is important because it highlights Leon's need to look after others, but also shows the importance of modelling- Leon knows how to comfort Sylvia because of how Sylvia comforted Leon in the past. Like he wants to replicate Tufty's cut off shorts and fashion sense, he learns to replicate Sylvia's approach to love. This highlights the nature vs nurture debate, and how important a child's upbringing and role models are for their development.

Example AQA-style question about the character of Sylvia

How does de Waal explore ideas about loyalty in *My Name is Leon*?
Write about:
- Where characters, such as Sylvia, demonstrate loyalty to others
- How de Waal presents ideas about loyalty

How does de Waal present Leon's relationship with Sylvia in *My Name is Leon*?
Write about:
- What Leon's relationship with Sylvia is like
- How de Waal presents Sylvia and Leon's relationship

Tufty

Tufty's Importance to the novel

With the lack of male role-models, and a situation which leaves Leon devoid of knowledge of his West Indian Heritage, Tufty quickly becomes a role model to Leon. He seems to enjoy teaching him and looking after him, and helps Leon to develop throughout the text. He seems to be an archetypal sage, and a ***paternal*** *(father-like)* figure.

Tufty's Key Moments

Chapters 16 and 17: Leon first sees Tufty on his bike, and then follows him into the allotments, immediately seeming to idolise him.

Chapter 18: Leon sees the posters of black power in Tufty's shed.

Chapter 20: Tufty plays dominoes with Mr Johnson, Castro, and his friends. Tufty tries to defuse the argument about protest by reading a funny poem called 'Conspiracy' about a girl, but Castro walks away in disgust thinking he's avoiding important issues.

Chapter 23: Lean listens to Tufty's music with him, and learns about dub music.

Chapter 27: Tufty and Castro are confronted in the allotments by the police. Police wreck Tufty's shed for no reason.

Chapter 29: Tufty argues with Devlin as Devlin and the committee want him out of the allotments. Tufty accuses Devlin of racism.

Chapter 30: Tufty shows Leon some Kung Fu moves, then gets angry about his treatment. He then gives a speech about his personal philosophy of peace.

Chapter 31: Tufty comes to the allotment when Castro has been hiding in his head, and shows concern for Leon which Leon enjoys.

Chapter 33- This is the chapter where Tufty reads his 'Ode to Castro' poem. Leon also learns about his ex-girlfriend and daughters.

Chapter 36- Tufty and Devlin have an argument about the protesters, and make mutual accusations about one another.

Chapters 37-40- After finding Leon in the shed and seeing him run into the protest, Tufty chases after him. He is beaten by a policeman as he tries to leave with Devlin and Leon, just because of his skin colout.

Chapter 42- At the end of the novel, Tufty helps set up the allotments for a street party. He and Devlin are now friends, and are still supporting Leon in the allotments.

Key Quotations

'His skin is brown [...] like his dad's but shiny and muscly like the Hulk. He has three scars across his shoulder like he's been shot or attacked, another scar on his cheek. He's a warrior.' (Ch. 17)

In his initial description of Tufty, Leon sees him as a '**wasp**' because of his yellow cycling clothes and dark skin. In Chapter 17, Leon's descriptions of him use the semantic field of strength and survival: '**hulk**', '**muscly**', and '**warrior**.' Leon immediately seems to idolise and admire him, and we sense the importance of him as a role model in Leon's life. The phrase 'warrior' is perhaps ironic as Tufty prefers peaceful protest, but de Waal could also be suggesting that there are different ways to fight for what you believe- not just violence.

'The sun,' he says, closing his eyes and turning his face to the sky, 'is a healer. When the sun comes out everybody smiles. World looks different. You can manage in the sun what you can't manage in the rain.' (Ch. 17)

This quotation is optimistic and hopeful. Like Maureen and Sylvia, Tufty tries to give the message that there are low points and high points in life, and when things are around you to support and nourish you, it's easier to feel positive.

'He folds the top of the seed packet over like he saw Tufty do and puts it in his pocket.' (Ch. 18)

Children learn by imitating adults, and copy what adults model. Leon lacks role models in his life, particularly male role models or those from his culture, and seems to see Tufty as a parent-figure. In the novel, Tufty seems to take on the Sage Archetype- he teaches Leon (about gardening, culture, and life in general), and has experience and wisdom.

'perhaps your balls haven't dropped yet, is that it?' (Ch. 27)

Even the police, when they approach Tufty, seem to be critical of his peaceful approach to the law, emasculating him and mocking him. It highlights issues about police mistreatment and prejudice, and in a society now where people are often praised for peaceful protest, seems unfair and cruel.

'This is about them police the other day. You see me do anything? You see me start any argument? I did nothing. [...]This is about racism, pure and simple.' (Ch. 29)

The reader recognises the unfariness of Tufty's treatment here- he did nothing wrong, but it being hounded by police and threatened for eviction from the allotments because of systemic racism. We empathise with Tufty here- he was criticised by the police for not doing anything in previous chapters, and now he's still facing negative consequences even when doing what he believes is right.

'When people f*** with you, you got a choice. You f*** back or you swallow down. [...] Swallow enough times and you start to choke. [...] Or you learn to accept. Let go. Breathe easy.' (Ch. 30)

This quotation seems to summarise Tufty's philosophy of life: you cannot get angry at things you cannot change (like Castro), but you need to accept and move on. We recognise here that people are faced with difficult choices when they witness or experience injustice. De Waal uses his changing perspectives on conflict to explore how we deal with difficult things.

'We are the consequence of history / We are the warriors you made.' 'We have dignity and worth.' (Ch. 33)

Perhaps in contrast to his personal philosophy we saw in Chapter 30, Tufty's poem emphasises how the history of Britain's treatment of black people- imperialism, slavery, the Windrush generation- has forced them into having to become warriors to fight back. The poem is powerful, and suggests a turning point in Tufty's character- he is no longer going to ignore or accept mistreatment, but will fight back through words and language.

'You ever been angry? [...] I mean down in your belly. You ever been angry in your balls?' (Chapter 36)

This quotation seems to epitomise the effects of mistreatment, oppression, and systemic racism: after Castro is killed by policemen in an unlawful moment of police brutality, Tufty has finally had enough of being peaceful and verbalises his anger at the injustice of the situation.

> 'I ain't fighting you, man. [...] I'm not a fighter. I don't hate people. I'm not fighting no more.' (Chapter 37)
>
> With the diversion of finding Leon, Tufty reverts back to his philosophy of peace. He is still angry, but recognises that there other ways to change rather than just violence.
>
> '**Leon likes it when they pretend to argue like they used to**.' (Chapter 42)
>
> This ending, where Devlin and Tufty are now friends, is a satisfactory <u>resolution</u> as one of the key conflicts of the <u>sub</u>-plot has now been resolved. It leaves the reader hopeful for the future.

<u>Example AQA-style questions about the character of Tufty</u>
Tufty says 'The sun [...] is a healer.' To what extent is *My Name is Leon* a story of hope and healing?
Write about:
- How characters feel hope and heal over the course of the novel
- How de Waal presents these ideas about hope and healing

Does de Waal present Tufty as an effective role model?
Write about:
- Where Tufty is and isn't an effective role model in the text
- How de Waal presents ideas about Tufty being a role model

How does de Waal use Tufty to explore ideas about protest in *My Name is Leon*?
Write about:
- What Tufty says and does
- How de Waal uses Tufty to explore ideas about protest

Devlin

Devlin's Importance to the novel

Devlin is one of the characters in the sub plot, and from the opening his past is wrapped up in mystery. Despite misgivings from Tufty about the intentions of his relationship with Leon, it transpires that he lost a son from a previous marriage because his son broke rules about running around traffic. This explains why Devlin is so focussed on keeping the rules. Devlin's ending is happy as he makes peace with Tufty and begins a relationship with Sylvia. His role as another <u>archetypal sage</u> in Leon's life is important, and his character reminds us how much the past can affect people's personalities.

Devlin's Key Moments

Chapter 17: Leon first sees Devlin arguing with Tufty. Devlin waves a knife towards Leon's neck, and argues about the rules of the allotment. As Leon leaves, he asks Devlin about his Kanetsune, but Devlin refuses to answer any more questions.

Chapter 18: As Leon leaves the allotments again, he speaks to Devlin who teaches him how to oil a knife. However, the reader feels uncomfortable at some of their conversations.

Chapter 26: In the allotments, Leon goes into Devlin's shed. There are lots of things that intrigue him, including many photographs of boys and wooden carvings.

Chapter 29: Devlin teaches Leon about plants, and when Leon says he wants to get stronger, Devlin takes him into his shed to give him some dumbbells. However, Tufty comes over and has an argument as Devlin is trying to evict him from the allotments- he believes it is racist discrimination, but Devlin denies it. When Tufty sees Leon in Devlin's shed, he insinuates Devlin is a paedophile. Leon steals a gun which the readers believe may be real, though it later turns out it's carved.

Chapter 31: Leon goes into Devlin's shed, but he's sleeping and drunk. When Leon tries to touch his knife, Devlin wakes up, and starts to carve Leon's head out of wood. He shows Leon his other carvings but falls asleep drunk again. After meeting Castro in Tufty's shed, Leon returns and steals whiskey, Devlin's favourite carved head, and a pruning knife.

Chapter 36: After the police and rioters trample through the allotments, Devlin and Tufty are arguing. Devlin wants Tufty to help fix the allotment gates to stop further damage, but in their argument Tufty accuses Devlin outright of being a paedophile. Devlin wants to explain things, but get really worked up, throwing things around in his shed looking for the carved head of his son, Gabriel, which Leon has in his rucksack. Tufty tries to calm him down.

Chapter 37: Devlin and Tufty find Leon hiding in his 'halfway house', and the head of Gabriel falls out of Leon's bag. Tufty tells Leon to apologise, but Leon rants about how everyone steals from him. Leon threatens them with the knife and leaves.

Chapter 39: Devlin has followed Leon into the riot, and reveals that the gun is wooden. He is hit in the attack, and falls to the floor. Tufty, Devlin, and Castro manage to escape through an alleyway.

Chapter 42: At the end of the book, Devlin is in a relationship with Sylvia. He has made friends with Tufty, and the ending is happy.

"'I used to be Señor Victor. Can you say Senhor Victor?' 'Senhor Victor.' Mr Devlin stares at Leon and then whispers, 'Or Papa.' 'Papa.' 'Ah,' says Mr Devlin." (Ch. 18)

This dialogue between Devlin and Leon might make the reader feel uncomfortable, as we do not know why Leon calling Devlin 'Papa' would make him sigh. At the end of the novel, we know that Devlin lost a son, but as the reader doesn't yet know this they might feel concerned about his intentions.

'photographs of boys, lots of them; dozens.' [...] 'there are things in Mr Devlin's shed that he wants to see again.' (Chapter 26)

The reader probably feels very uncomfortable here, wondering why Devlin has lots of pictures of boys in his shed. They might feel concern for Leon who wants to see his items, and worry that Leon doesn't have any suspicions towards Devlin.

'Stay away from that man. He don't like black people unless they're under sixteen.' (Ch. 29)

Tufty's concerns about Devlin's intentions may echo the readers'. However, Devlin has done nothing that Tufty hasn't done, for example inviting him into his shed, giving him things, teaching, and talking.

'Keep the f***ing rules! Isn't that what I told him? Isn't it? Slow down, I said. Over and over, I said it. […] Don't run!' […] It's my fault, she said. My fault for shouting. He wasn't looking. My fault. Always my fault. Always will be my fault. For ever and ever. Amen.' (Ch. 31)
Here, the true tragedy of Devlin is revealed: he was unable to prevent the death of his son. A lot of his behaviours are given context, for example his desire to talk to Leon and his need for rules. We feel sympathy for Devlin here.
'It's a protest. Except we don't bomb people in their beds like you Irish people.' […] 'Oh, every Irishman is a terrorist, is that what you're saying?' (Ch. 36)
Here, xenophobic attitudes towards the Irish and stereotypes are raised. It is ironic that both Devlin and Tufty mistreat each other because of negative stereotypes.
'Leon likes it when they pretend to argue like they used to.' (Ch. 42)
At the end of the novel, we can see how Leon's relationship with Tufty and Devlin has led to a resolution; they are both happy friends, and even their faux arguments remind Leon of how far they have come.

Example AQA-style questions about the character of Devlin
Devlin says 'Oh, every Irishman is a terrorist, is that what you're saying?' How does de Waal explore ideas about stereotypes in *My Name is Leon*.
Write about:
- How characters are stereotyped in the text
- How de Waal presents ideas about stereotypes

D – Example Essay

How does de Waal present Leon's relationships with the adults in his life?

Write about:
- What Leon's relationship is like with different adults in his life
- How de Waal presents the relationship between Leon and the adults in his life.

In de Waal's 2016 bildungsroman, <u>My Name is Leon</u>, we see that Leon has both positive and negative relationships with various adults in his life. However, it seems to be his relationships with Maureen, Tufty, and the Zebra that are the most instrumental in his development. De Waal might have presented Leon's relationships with adults as so pivotal in his life to remind the reader of the importance of adult role models in helping a child grow into an adult. De Waal presents Leon's relationship with Maureen as a positive one: she cares for him and nurtures him. De Waal associates Maureen with religious imagery- she has pictures of Jesus on her wall	**INTRODUCTION:** **Introduce text, task, and argument.** Introduces the text, considering the genre of the novel (see page 36). Introduces the main topics of the essay- in this case, the three characters that will be explored. **Thesis Statement:** The argument that will run throughout the essay. In this case, the argument is about WHY relationships are so important. This includes tentative language (p. 42) **BODY PARAGRAPHS:** These explore WHAT, HOW, and WHY- in this case, WHAT relationships are like, HOW de Waal presents relationships like this, and WHY.

144

and Leon says, in his first day with her, that her hair 'glows like a halo.' This religious imagery emphasises that, even from the first moment Leon sees Maureen, he sees her a saviour. The simile of Maureen's hair being like a 'halo' presents Maureen as an angel, and the verb 'glows' is positive. Throughout the novel, Maureen is presented as the archetypal caregiver, emphasised by the motif of food- Leon's first night with her is characterised by biscuits, and his first morning by bacon sandwiches. De Waal uses the motif of the 'golden biscuit tin' to emphasise how nurturing Maureen is- a foil character to the neglectful Carol whose inability to care for Leon left him 'malnourished.' De Waal could have used Maureen as a foil to the character of Carol to make the reader question what makes a good mother, as Maureen is more stereotypically maternal than Carol ever was shown to be. Perhaps this is why Maureen and Leon's relationship is so positive.

References can include both quotations and details from the text.

Analysis can include word and sentence level analysis, but also whole text analysis: in this paragraph, the candidate zooms in the significance of the simile and key words, but also looks at how Maureen is presented as an archetypal character and how she is used as a foil character. See page 144.

Here, the candidate is zooming out to think about WHY the character might have been presented this way- what bigger concepts and themes are illuminated?

De Waal also presents Leon's relationship with Tufty as a positive one; Leon looks up to him. When Leon first sees Tufty, he describes him as 'like the hulk', 'muscly' and says 'He's a warrior.' The semantic field of strength is used to describe him, and the reader recognises that, without any male role models in his life (his father being in prison), Leon sees Tufty as a paternal role model. Furthermore, as an archetypal sage, we see that Tufty teaches Leon and guides him: he encourages Leon to read to him, teaches him about 'dub' and West Indian heritage, and shows him the posters of black power icons on his shed. The setting of the allotments is symbolic because they represent growth; Tufty helps Leon to become a man. Indeed, at the end of the novel when Leon is facing a police officer in the riot, it is Leon's quoting of Tufty's poem ('We are not a warrior [...] We have dignity and worth') that seems to save his life; the policeman lets him go. The reader recognises that,	**Topic sentence:** the first sentence of each paragraph should include the author's name, the key words from the question, and summarise the focus for that paragraph.

as a biracial boy, Leon needs to see positive role models that look like him, and this may therefore be why de Waal shows Tufty and Leon as having such a positive relationship.

However, de Waal seems to summarise what makes adult and child relationships effective through the character of The Zebra. Leon recognises that 'Out of all the social workers he's ever had, she looks at him the most', emphasising a child's need to be seen and understood. She is a juxtaposition to the Earring, who 'asks all the questions the Zebra asks but faster, writing and talking or putting ticks in boxes' — Leon is almost like a literal 'tick boxing' exercise for him; he doesn't care about the child in front of him or get to know him. The Zebra, on the other hand, recognises his need for independence and freedom, bringing him the BMX bike which enables him to go to the allotments and meet Tufty and Devlin. De Waal worked as a magistrate for social care, and

Closing sentence: Again, use the author's name and the key words from the question in the last sentence of every body paragraph.

Discourse Markers: Connectives and other linking statements are used to create a sense of development in the argument, always linking to the thesis.

Context is embedded, and only linked to the topic of the essay (see page 117).

has said in an interview that often children in social care don't have a voice. The Zebra recognises that he does have a voice and individual needs, which is what makes their relationship so important in Leon's life.

In conclusion, de Waal seems to present Leon's relationships with adults in his life as varied and mixed- some relationships, that like with the Earring, are negative and expose criticisms about the social system. Leon's relationship with Carol is also conflicted, because of her inability to look after him and be a traditional mother. However, de Waal suggests that what makes relationships with children and adults so effective is when adults take the time to truly see and understand children, like Maureen and the Zebra. It's also important that children are exposed to a variety of role models, including those who look like them and share his cultural background.

CONCLUSION: Consider the writer's intentions- WHY did de Waal want to present the topic or character in this way?

Essay Hint- Writer's Methods (AO2)

When writing essays, it's important to look at the writer's choices at word and sentence level, as well as choices at whole text level.

Word and Sentence Level:
- **Effects of key words** (connotations and denotations, tone of words)
- **Sensory Imagery** (visual, olfactory, kinaesthetic, tactile, auditory, gustatory)
- **Figurative language** (similes, metaphors, personification)
- **Other language devices** (onomatopoeia, alliteration, imagery)
- **Syntax** (sentence structure such as anaphora, sentence type)
- Choice of **dialogue, action, or description**

Whole Text Level:
- **Setting**
- **Themes**
- **Atmosphere**
- **Symbol**
- **Juxtaposition** (and any other contrasts created)
- **Motif**
- **Character** (archetypes, foils)
- **Genre-** (bildungsroman, coming of age, own voices)
- **Narrative Voice** (third person limited perspective)
- **Structure-** (the order in which we learn things, and how each chapter and event has been structured; flashback, flashforward, shifts in time)

E- Glossary

Allusion- A reference to a famous person, setting, event or work. Allusions can be direct or indirect.

Anaphoric Listing- Repeating words / phrases at the start of successive clauses

Anticipation- The expectation of something big happening, or a climax occurring

Aptronymic- A name which suits the characters' characteristics.

Archetype- An idea, character, symbol or pattern that appears in stories around the world regardless of culture and team. It seems to symbolise something universal about the human experience.
- Caregiver- A character who is selfless and sacrificing, supporting and caring for others.
- Innocent- Someone who is naïve and unexperienced about the world around them
- Sage- A wise person who mentors those they meet and teachers them about the world

Character- A person in a literary work

Cliff-hanger- Ending a chapter or section on a moment of high tension

Colloquial- Chatty / conversational

Coming-of-Age- A genre (also known as a bildungsroman) which narrates the story of a protagonist from childhood to adulthood; immaturity to maturity; naïve to wise.

Contrast- Something opposing / opposite

Dark humour- A style of comedy that makes light of serious subject matter

Dialogue- Speech

Direct Address- Speaking to someone personally with the pronoun 'you'

Ellipsis- Three dots (...) used to show that there are elements to the sentence missing

Euphemism- A more polite way of saying something rude, controversial, or upsetting

Exposition- The opening of a novel, where information about key characters and settings is established.

Figurative Language- Anything that's not literal, such as similes and metaphors

Foil- A character who serves as a contrast to another character, to highlight particular aspect of their character

Foreboding- A sense that something bad will happen.

Foreshadowing- Hints about what will happen later on the text

Graphic Imagery- Something described in shocking detail, often with blood or gore.

Imperative- A command verb (in KS2 we call these 'bossy verbs')

Inference- A conclusion based on logic and reasoning. As a reader, we infer things from what the writer implies.

Irony- Using language that signals the opposite, usually for comedic or emphatic effect.

Juxtaposition- A contrast between two things

List- A number of connected things listed consecutively

Metaphor- Direct Comparison

Motif- A feature, idea, or image that reoccurs throughout a text to develop other narrative elements such as theme or mood.

Narrative- Story

Oxymoron- Two contrasting things next to each other

Pathetic Fallacy- The weather / environment reflects the emotions of the characters / the atmosphere of the text

Polysyndeton- A list using multiple conjunctions (connectives)

Profanity – Swearing

Protagonist- Main character

Pun- A joke with a play on words

Semantic Field- A group of connected words

Sensory Imagery- Words which evoke any of the senses. Sensory imagery can include: Visual Imagery (Sight); Auditory Imagery (Sound); Olfactory Imagery (Smell); Gustatory Imagery (Taste); Tactile Imagery (Touch).

Simile- An indirect comparison, usually using 'like' or 'as' to compare the qualities of one thing to another.

Slang- Informal language

Subplot- A secondary story that happens alongside the main plot.

Symbolism- A symbol is where something represents something else in a text.

Tension- Building conflict for the characters

Theme- Underlying messages or deeper meanings that the writer explores in literary texts.

Third Person Limited Point of View- The writer tells the story from the perspective of the protagonist; the reader sees the thoughts of the protagonist, but through the third person 'he' or 'she'.

<u>Tone</u>- The author's attitude towards a certain topic

Printed in Great Britain
by Amazon